Alone with Others
An Existential Approach to Buddhism

The Faith to Doubt
Glimpses of Buddhist Uncertainty

The Awakening of the West
The Encounter of Buddhism and Western Culture

Buddhism Without Beliefs
A Contemporary Guide to Awakening

Verses from the Center
A Buddhist Vision of the Sublime

LIVING

WITH

THE DEVIL

A MEDITATION ON
GOOD AND EVIL

Stephen Batchelor

RIVERHEAD BOOKS

a member of Penguin Group (USA) Inc.

New York

2004

Riverhead Books
a member of
Penguin Group (USA) Inc.
375 Hudson Street
New York, NY 10014

Library of Congress Cataloging-in-Publication Data

Batchelor, Stephen.
Living with the devil : a meditation on good and evil / Stephen Batchelor.
p.   cm.
Includes bibliographical references.
ISBN 1-57322-276-3
1. Religious life—Buddhism.   2. Good and evil—
Religious aspects—Buddhism.   3. Buddhism—Doctrines.   I. Title.
BQ4301.B37   2004   2004042759
294.3'5—dc22

Printed in the United States of America
1   3   5   7   9   10   8   6   4   2

This book is printed on acid-free paper. ⊚

Book design by Chris Welch

For Hay

CONTENTS

I do not know who put me in the world, nor what the world is, nor what I am myself. I am in a terrible ignorance about everything. I do not know what my body is, or my senses, or my soul, or even that part of me which thinks what I am saying, which reflects on itself and everything but knows itself no better than anything else. I see the terrifying spaces of the universe enclosing me, and I find myself attached to one corner of this expanse without knowing why I have been placed here rather than there, or why the life allotted me should be assigned to this moment [rather] than to another in all the eternity that preceded and will follow me. I see only infinity on every side, enclosing me like an atom or a shadow that vanishes in an instant.

—BLAISE PASCAL

ONE

THE GOD OF THIS AGE

1

Parallel Mythologies

THIS IS A BOOK for those like myself who find themselves living in the gaps between different and sometimes con-
flicting mythologies—epic narratives that help us make sense
of this brief life on earth. Some of these mythologies originate
in distant times and places, while others are products of the
modern world.

Whether the myths we inherit from the past come from a
monotheistic religion such as Judaism or Christianity or a non-
theistic tradition such as Buddhism, they share the view that a
human life is fully intelligible only as part of an immense cosmic
drama that transcends it. Both believe hidden powers to be at
work—whether of God or karma makes little difference—
that have flung us into this world to face the daunting task of
redeeming ourselves for the remainder of eternity.

The myths of modernity are so close at hand that it is hard to recognize them as myths. Just as those who lived in a premodern Christian or Buddhist society did not regard their understanding of the world as mythological, we too fail to see the mythologies that underpin our sense of who we are and the kind of universe we inhabit. A dominant myth of modernity is provided by the scientific understanding of the world that has blossomed in the West during the past two centuries. So compelling is its account of the origins of the universe and sentient life, so awesome its explanatory and predictive power, so impressive the technologies made possible by its understanding of the physical world, that we refuse to acknowledge anything mythical about it at all.

Even if what we believe is empirically verifiable, that does not prevent it from functioning as a myth. No matter how "true" the modern scientific worldview may be, it plays a similar role in our lives today as prescientific worldviews played in the lives of those in premodern cultures. For it too explains how human life is only fully intelligible as part of an immense cosmic drama that transcends it. It too is sustained by beliefs. We believe the universe exploded out of nothing fifteen billion years ago; we believe that humans evolved by random selection of genetic mutations from more primitive forms of life; we believe in the existence of electrons and quarks. But would we be able to demonstrate the truth of any one of these claims to someone who did *not* believe them?

Human knowledge is invariably limited and partial. There is only so much any one person, however intelligent and well informed, can reasonably claim to know with certainty. Whatever he knows is necessarily mediated through his instruments, his senses, his reason, his brain. It is impossible for him to have access to an unmediated vantage point independent of his instruments and apart from his organism whence he could check to see whether his mediated knowledge corresponds to reality as such. No matter how well it can be explained, reality remains essentially mysterious. And on the great questions of what it means to be born and die, do good and evil, the natural sciences are silent.

But the old ancestral myths run deep. We continue to draw on them for answers to such questions. The avowed atheist and materialist is uncomfortably stirred by passages from the Bible. The convert to Buddhism discovers a more intimate sense of the sacred in a crumbling village church in England than in all the monasteries she has visited in Tibet. In moments of despair, neither can help calling out to the god they have abandoned.

As a Westerner who has practiced Buddhism for the past thirty years, I am aware of the parallel mythologies within me that compete for my attention. I was not raised a Christian, but recognize how I have imbibed the myths and values of Christianity from the post-Christian, liberal humanist environment around me. Temperamentally, I incline more to the arts than the sciences, but I thrill to the emerging scientific worldview that informs the society of which I am a part. My entire adult life has been devoted to translating Buddhist texts, teaching Buddhist meditation and philosophy, and writing books that offer a contemporary interpretation of Buddhism. As I struggle to understand and articulate the teachings and myths of my adopted faith, I am continually aware of other voices I equally cherish.

At the heart of Buddha's awakening lies a counterintuitive recognition of human experience as radically transient, unreliable, and contingent. By paying sustained, unsentimental attention to life as it unfolded within and around him, Siddhattha Gotama (the historical Buddha) realized that no essential self either underpinned or stood back and viewed the integrated display of colors, shapes, sounds, sensations, thoughts, and feelings that arise and vanish in each moment of consciousness. This startling insight shook him to the core of what he felt himself to be. The instinctive conviction of being an unchanging, isolated "I" collapsed. Life was just a dazzlingly tentative array of contingent processes, playing themselves out in complex sequences of causes and effects but with no discernible beginning and no divine power mysteriously directing them to a preordained end.

Gotama found this revelation of a selfless and Godless reality to be deeply liberating. He was freed from the self-centered compulsions and fears that had trapped him in seemingly endless cycles of boredom and anguish. He referred to this freedom as "nirvana"—literally a "blowing out" of the "fires" of such existential discontent. Elsewhere, he spoke of this as "emptiness": an open space where the idea of being an isolated and permanent self is no longer able to ensnare one. This emptiness is "the abode of a great person," where one can encounter and respond to the world from a selfless but caring perspective.

A bleak, nihilistic void in which meaning and value have been lost is the exact opposite of what Buddha meant by "emptiness." For him, an understanding of emptiness transformed a compulsive cycle of fears and cravings into a path of wisdom and care that enhanced inner freedom and empathetic responsiveness. Rather than an absence of meaning and value, emptiness is an absence of what limits and confines one's capacity to realize what a human life can potentially become.

As soon as emptiness is thought of as a subtle dimension of reality or a mystical state of mind, it risks becoming fetishized as another privileged religious object. Nagarjuna, the great second century Indian thinker, was acutely aware of this danger:

> *Buddhas say emptiness*
> *Is relinquishing opinions.*
> *Believers in emptiness*
> *Are incurable.*

Emptiness is not something sacred in which to believe. It is an *emptying:* a letting go of the fixations and compulsions that lock one into a tight cell of self that seems to exist in detached isolation from the turbulent flux of life. This emptying leads to a falling away of constrictive and obstructive habits of mind that—as in removing a barrier across a river—allows the dammed-up torrent of life to flow freely.

Letting go, even momentarily and unintentionally, of that desperate and obsessive grip on self does not obliterate you but opens you up to a fleeting and highly contingent world that you share with other anxious creatures like yourself. This can be frightening; for the only certainty in such a world is that at some point you will die. You realize that your self is not a fixed thing or personal essence but a tentative and confused story hastening toward its conclusion. This might prompt you to scurry back to the familiar perceptions, beliefs, and routines in which you feel secure. But once the process of emptying has started, to cling to such consolations will hinder you from feeling fully alive. To become empty, as Nagarjuna insists, is to encounter the raw, unfiltered contingency of life itself. The challenge of emptiness is to plunge into life's torrent rather than hover uncertainly on its brink.

"Contingency" is a concise and reasonably accurate translation of the Buddhist concept *paticcasamuppada* (usually rendered as "dependent origination"). Whatever is contingent depends on something else for its existence. As such, it *need* not have happened. For had one of those conditions failed to materialize, something else would have occurred. We make "contingency" plans because life is full of surprises, and no matter how careful our preparations, things often do not turn out as anticipated. The devilish complexity of living systems makes it hard to foresee how a given system (be it a person or a flock of birds) will behave in the next moment, let alone next month or next year. Contingency reveals a chaotic freedom at the heart of causally ordered events. However tempting it is to invoke the hand of God, karma, or destiny to inject a hidden order into what seems random, embracing contingency requires a willingness to accept the inexplicable and unpredictable instead of reaching for the anesthetic comfort of metaphysics.

The opposite of "contingency" is "necessity." No matter how ephemeral and insignificant I recognize this human life of mine to be, I cannot shake off an intuitive conviction that, deep down, my existence is necessary in the scheme of things. By paying close and sustained attention to the contingent nature of experience, the practice of Buddhist meditation challenges the instinctive feeling that we are, in the words of Milton's Satan, "self-begot, self-raised / By our own quick'ning power." In eroding this sense of our own necessity, we come to see how the unprecedented and unrepeatable person we are emerges from a sublime matrix of myriad contingent events—no one of which *need* have happened either. Insight into the emptiness of self is achieved not by eliminating self but by understanding it to be contingent rather than necessary.

When the stubborn, frozen solidity of necessary selves and things is dissolved in the perspective of emptiness, a contingent world opens up that is fluid and ambiguous, fascinating and terrifying. Not only does this world unfold before us with awesome subtlety, complexity, and majesty, one day it will swallow us up in its tumultuous wake along with everything else we cherish. The infinitely poignant beauty of creation is inseparable from its diabolic destructiveness. How to live in such a turbulent world with wisdom, tolerance, empathy, care, and nonviolence is what saints and philosophers have struggled over the centuries to articulate. What is striking about the Buddhist approach is that rather than positing an immortal or transcendent self that is immune to the vicissitudes of the world, Buddha insisted that salvation lies in discarding such consoling fantasies and embracing instead the very stuff of life that will destroy you.

This book is a meditation on some of these age-old questions. Much of it is an interpretation of Buddhist myths, doctrines, philosophy, and practice. Yet as one who finds himself inhabiting the gaps between cultures and traditions, the Buddhist ideas are juxtaposed and interwoven with material from sources as diverse as the Bible, Baudelaire, Roland Barthes, and evolutionary biology. Although I cite the monotheistic scriptures, I do not believe in God any more than I believe in Hamlet. But this does not mean that either God or Hamlet has nothing of value to say. The pages of this book are populated with mythical and historical figures from various traditions who happen to speak to my condition. The path I trace follows the gaps between different religious and secular mythologies that help make sense of my life. The further I proceed, the more I suspect this path to be nothing but the anarchic gaps themselves.

2

This Need Not Have Happened

I WAS ABOUT SIXTEEN when my mother inadvertently undermined the instinctive conviction that my existence was necessary. It was Christmas. She and her sister were leafing through a volume of photographs on the kitchen table. They came to a snapshot of a man in military fatigues—eyes squinting against the desert sun, pipe clenched between teeth. Mother said, "If things had worked out differently, he would have been your father." I thought: *If he had been my father, would I have been me?*

This adolescent glimpse of my own contingency has haunted me. In spite of an intuitive conviction that my presence in this world is somehow necessary, the treacherous and unsettling possibility that I need not have happened at all keeps gnawing away. Leaving aside her choice of suitor, had another of my actual father's myriad spermatozoa impregnated my mother's ovum, would the child born from such a mingling of chromosomes have been me? Or had the same spermatozoon burrowed home in her next ovarian cycle, would that baby have been me?

Or had the policeman's gun that fired the bullet that killed Erwin von Scheubner-Richter on November 9, 1923, been angled fractionally to the right, it would have struck the man whose arm was linked to his: Adolf Hitler. Had Hitler died at that moment, my mother and the man she might have married would almost certainly not have met in the North African desert. The same shot would likewise have scrambled in unforeseeable ways the myriad circumstances, choices, and events that led her to meet my actual father some years later.

To dwell on the improbability of spending seventy-odd years on this planet as one of six billion worrying apes upsets the consoling belief that deep down inside I am a permanent and independent soul. Yet as long as I can remember, this same me has gazed out faithfully and unwaveringly onto a world of other things and people from its solitary aerie concealed inside this flesh. The person whose story begins with a memory of sitting on a woman's lap, nestling in the folds of her fur coat while peering through an airplane window at the miniature houses and cars of Toronto, seems to be the very one who is writing these words now.

In an abstract and ineffectual manner, I know this cannot be true. For I have grown up and changed. I can no longer identify with either my three-year-old body or three-year-old mind.

Physically, emotionally, and mentally I have become someone else. But I cannot help feeling that I am the same person who wiggled that child's chubby fingers and reveled in its infant delights. Yet as soon as I turn my attention toward this indisputably real person, he slips away. He vanishes.

I did not choose to be here, but now I cannot accept the thought of not being here. However certain I feel about the necessity of my existence, the only certainty I face is that this seemingly necessary being will perish. This heart will cease pumping blood, these lungs will cease drawing air, these neurons will cease firing in my brain. My body will rot or be consumed by fire, and within a matter of years I will linger on by the slenderest of threads as a memory in the fading minds of those who once knew me. And when they are gone, only photographs and marks I made on paper and computer discs will remain. Then these traces too will turn to dust.

I avoid such thoughts by keeping my attention firmly focused on getting through the business of daily life. Or rather, an instinctive urge to survive keeps my attention focused on this task. For even when I stop to meditate on the contingency and transience of this existence, I find myself repeatedly torn away by other thoughts and feelings that clamor for attention. I do not want to be distracted from my contemplation, but I find it hard to resist the urge to be elsewhere. At such moments, my entire organism seems subject to compulsions I can barely control. In spite of myself, I am drawn away from an awareness of the contingent flux of life and back to the cell of self-centered preoccupation.

When Dante enters hell's ninth and final circle, he finds himself on the edge of a vast plain of ice. He heads off into a dark, cold wind to discover Satan submerged to his chest in the ice, flapping his six batlike wings. In contrast to the fiery upper circles of hell, where beings suffer tortures cruelly fashioned after their sins, "the king of the vast kingdom of all grief" is frozen and trapped. Likewise, my restless fears and longings feel as though they are governed by a tyrannical self that seems frozen at my core. It is here that the denial of life's contingency and the insistence on my own necessity are most intensely experienced. Dante's descent into hell suggests that the closer you come to the heart of the demonic, the more you are deprived of light and warmth. You experience alienation and despair. Hell is a metaphor of desolation.

But the devil is more than just a figurative way of describing a compulsive reaction to this contingent world into which we were thrown at birth. There is something demonic about the contingent world itself. This is a place where things we don't want to happen, happen. Cars skid on ice and swerve off roads into trees instead of reaching their destination. Floods, bombs, and earthquakes destroy in moments what years of labor have created. At times I feel hemmed in on all sides: inwardly subjected to the urges of an organism that is programmed to survive, outwardly overwhelmed by the tragedy of a suffering world. No matter how sincerely and passionately I choose to do good, I keep doing the opposite. I make a declaration of my most deeply held values, only to find myself furtively betraying them. I take a vow to dedicate myself to the welfare of others, but remain resolutely committed to my own well-being.

"I yearn to be free of pain," wrote the eighth-century Indian Buddhist Shantideva, "but rush straight into it; I long for happiness, but foolishly crush it like an enemy." A thousand years later, Pascal noted how "we desire truth and find in ourselves nothing but uncertainty. We seek happiness and find only misery and death." Such contradictoriness is more than an occasional moral lapse that could be corrected by the fear of punishment or a timely boost of righteousness. It appears to be knit into the fabric of existence itself.

Even when a calm, authoritative voice whispers that I am contradicting myself by indulging a compulsion, why do I find it so hard to desist? It is as if a relentless power is driving me toward an inescapable fate. Part of me feels hypnotized, as if it is sleepwalking, under a spell, addicted to a sensation it cannot renounce. I know why I shouldn't be doing what I am, but can't seem to help it. The struggle to resist temptation is like the struggle to resist the pull of a tide. And these longings seem but pale shadows of that deeper and darker drift of our existence, which is known as the devil.

3

Mara—The Killer

IN POPULAR MYTHOLOGY, devils are quixotic and cruel tyrants who relish tormenting their victims. Their vitality obscures how the demonic is subjectively experienced as a state of existential and psychological paralysis. When seized by a demon, one feels suffocated, oppressed, and fatigued as one struggles to be free from what entraps one. The devil is a way of talking about that which blocks one's path in life, frustrates one's aspirations, makes one feel stuck, hemmed in, obstructed. While the Hebrew *Satan* means "adversary," the Greek *diabolos* means "one who throws something across the path." In India, Buddha called the devil *Mara,* which in Pali and Sanskrit means "the killer."

In an early discourse entitled *The Striving,* Gotama recalls,

I was living on the bank of the Neranjara River en-
gaged in deep struggle, practicing meditation with all
my strength in the effort to find freedom. Then Mara
came up to me and started talking in words appearing to
be full of sympathy: "You are so thin and pale," he said.
"You must be nearly dead. It would be far better to live.
You could do much good by leading a holy life."

The devil appears to have Buddha's best interests at heart. At
first glance, what he says seems reasonable. Mara discourages
Buddha's asceticism and extols a life dedicated to doing good
in the world. He does not encourage Gotama to do anything
evil. His aim is to weaken his resolve to be free from the compulsive drives that trap him in cycles of anguish.

While speaking to Gotama, Mara "stood right next to Buddha." The devil insinuates himself in such a way that he seems
to be part of Buddha's own thinking. But Buddha recognizes
him, saying,

I see your troops all around me, Mara, but I will proceed
with the struggle. Even if the whole world cannot defeat
your army, I will destroy it with the power of wisdom
just as an unfired pot is smashed by a stone.

To show his potency, Mara is depicted as a warlord mounted
on an elephant, commanding a legion of troops. Buddha did
not consider "any power so hard to conquer as the power of

Mara." He enumerates the armies under Mara's command as sensual desire, discontent, hunger and thirst, craving, lethargy, fear, doubt, restlessness, longing for gain, praise, honor and fame, and extolling oneself while disparaging others. Gotama tells of how he struggled to be free from these forces that seemed to besiege and attack him, blur his vision, darken his understanding, and thus divert him from his goal of freedom.

Identifying with a desire or a fear tightens the knot that binds one to it and, thereby, the sway it can have over one. Only when Buddha was able to experience the desires and fears that threatened to overwhelm him as nothing but impersonal and ephemeral conditions of mind and body, did they lose their power to mesmerize him. Instead of perceiving them as forces of an avenging army intent on his destruction, he recognized that they were no more solid than brittle, unfired pots that crumble on being struck by a well-aimed stone. As soon as Buddha stopped compulsively identifying the thoughts, feelings, and sensations that arose within him as "me" or "mine," Mara could no longer influence him.

This does not mean that Buddha was either unaware of these thoughts and feelings or that they no longer occurred for him. Rather than deleting them, he discovered a way of being with them in which they could gain no purchase on him. Mara describes this with an analogy:

> I remember once seeing a crow hovering above a lump
> of fat on the ground. "Food!" it thought. But the lump

turned out to be a rock, hard and inedible; the crow flew away in disgust. I too have had enough; I'm like that crow pecking at a rock; I am finished with Gotama.

Buddha makes himself immune to Mara. No matter how much Mara tries to inveigle his way into his mind, Buddha remains calm and equanimous. He inhabits that free and selfless space that is outside of Mara's range. He is one "whom Mara cannot overcome, any more than the winds can overcome the Himalaya." Buddha compares someone who "has deprived Mara's eye of its opportunity" to a deer wandering at ease in the remote depths of a forest, who "walks without fear, stands without fear, sits without fear, lies down without fear." For, having "blindfolded Mara," he becomes "invisible" to the devil. Mara, however, compares himself to a crab whose limbs have been torn off by children. He says to Buddha: "All those distortions, manoeuvres, and contortions of mine have been cut off, broken, and smashed to bits by you."

Unless we are prepared to regard the devil as a ghostly apparition who sits down and has conversations with Buddha, we cannot but understand him as a metaphoric way of describing Buddha's own inner life. Although Buddha is said to have "conquered" the forces of Mara on achieving awakening, that did not prevent Mara from harassing him until shortly before his death fifty years later. Mara's tireless efforts to undermine Buddha by accusing him of insincerity, self-deception, idleness, arrogance, and aloofness are ways of describing the doubts within Buddha's own mind.

Mara stands for those patterns of behavior that long for the security of clinging to something real and permanent rather than facing the question posed by being a transient and contingent creature. "It makes no difference what you grasp," said Buddha, "when someone grasps, Mara stands beside him." Mara is that desperate longing for a self and a world that are comprehensible, manageable, and safe. Such clinging, however, turns into a kind of death. As its hold tightens, one feels as though life itself is being stifled and snuffed out. Mara is sometimes called Namuci, the drought demon of Vedic mythology, whose name means "one who withholds the waters." The hold that Mara exerts blocks the flow of life just as Namuci's grip prevents the monsoon from unleashing its waters.

In response to Mara's provocations, Buddha says, "I know you, evil one. Do not think otherwise." The devil is conquered not by forcibly expelling him but by understanding his strategies and seeing through his charade of invincibility. Experiential insight into the nature of Mara is the key to freeing oneself from his grip. Buddha was able to overcome Mara by stabilizing his attention sufficiently in meditation to be able to see clearly and deeply into the nature of the demonic powers that assailed him. Once he understood exactly what he was up against, he could no longer be tricked by Mara's hypnotic and seductive gaze.

As soon as Mara realizes that Buddha understands him and is inaccessible to him, he departs. "Mara was so upset by his failure," says *The Striving*, "that he dropped his guitar and the moment it fell to the ground he disappeared." Elsewhere, "Mara shook his head, lolled his tongue, knit his brow into three furrows, and departed leaning on his staff." On another occasion, he

> went away from that spot and sat down cross-legged on the ground not far from Buddha, silent, dismayed, with his shoulders drooping, downcast, brooding, unable to speak, scratching the ground with a stick.

With his guard down, Mara is tragically human. He might have stepped out of the pages of a novel. In contrast, Buddha tends to be rather distant. He commands respect, but rarely allows a glimpse of his humanity. Mara may be duplicitous and parasitic, but in the acceptance of his failings he is oddly endearing. We sense something of ourself in him.

Mara approaches Buddha as "a farmer, carrying a large plough on his shoulder, holding a long goad stick, his hair disheveled, wearing hempen garments, his feet smeared with mud." He takes the form of a brahmin, "with a large matted topknot, clad in an antelope hide, old, crooked like a roof bracket, wheezing, holding a staff of udumbara wood." The bedraggled farmer and wheezing brahmin embody the sensuality of the natural world. When Buddha exposes him as Mara, the farmer retorts, "The eyes are mine. Shapes and colors are mine. Their impact on the eyes is mine. Consciousness is mine. Where can you go to escape me?" Mara saturates every nook and cranny of life. Not only is he everything one sees, hears, tastes, smells, touches, and thinks, but he is also the acts of seeing, hearing, tasting, smelling, touching, and thinking themselves. Mara draws us under his spell through the fascination and terror of the natural world.

As a warm-blooded, breathing, conscious creature, Gotama is intimate with Mara. Yet he knows Mara, has conquered Mara, and is immune to Mara. "Where there are no eyes, no shapes or colors, no impact with them and no consciousness of them," he says in response to the farmer's question, "there is no place for you there, evil one." Buddha escapes Mara by abiding in emptiness: that open spaciousness of mind where fantasies of being a fearful and isolated self no longer ensnare him. He is fully in the world but no longer fooled by the way things appear as discrete units designed to attract or repel him. Mara has no place in this emptiness because he is the one who both conjures up and sustains the illusion of the segregated specifics of life.

In order to "arouse fear, trepidation and terror" in Buddha, Mara harnesses the forces of nature herself. He detonates explosions that sound "as though the earth were splitting open." He shatters boulders near Buddha, he appears as a giant elephant, a king cobra, and an ox. Mara is the natural world in all its glory and horror. This very earth that can leave you dumb with wonder as you contemplate its selfless unfolding will destroy you with neither malice nor mercy should its tectonic plates shift beneath your feet. Sublimely indifferent to our hopes and fears, life snuffs us out at death no matter how tenaciously we cling to it.

Mara means "the killer." Mara is the Grim Reaper. In Tibet, he is depicted as Yama, lord of death, holding the world between his teeth, ready to clamp shut at any moment. The devil is the precariousness of existence, its unreliability, its arbitrariness. Shortly before Buddha's death, Mara pays him a final visit. "You have accomplished everything that you set out to do," he says, "Your teaching and community are well established. Your legacy is assured. Now please die and enter the final nirvana." Rather than rebuke him, Buddha says, "You need not worry, evil one. The Tathagata's passing will not be long delayed." Gotama knows the game is up. Mara neither slinks away in despair nor drops his guitar and disappears.

Buddha calls Mara the *Antaka*. While *anta* means "end," "limit," "boundary," or "horizon," the Pali suffix *-ka* implies "one who makes" or "imposes" such things. Mara is that which limits us, confines us within boundaries, fixes our horizons, and brings everything to an end. Not only are we limited by what our physical body allows us to do and ultimately by its death, we are constrained by other boundaries that are neither unavoidable nor necessary. We inherit or adopt opinions about ourselves and the world that we cling to and refuse to relinquish. So certain are we of being "right" that our convictions feel embedded in our flesh. Yet, to be ensnared by them locks us into fixed dogmatic positions, which are a form of intellectual and spiritual death.

Mara stands for sex as well as death. He is both the yearning to conceive life and that which brings it to an end. Sexual desire has such deep biological roots that, of all Mara's troops, it assails us most forcibly. Only after Mara has failed in his attempts to influence Buddha do his three daughters approach their despondent, doodling father and promise to "catch Buddha with the snare of lust." They offer themselves to Buddha in every imaginable female form, but he remains unmoved. For an ordinary mortal to have resisted such an erotic assault would, they reflect, have produced either cardiac arrest or insanity. Only the impotent would be unmoved. While Buddha remains alert to the urges of his biology as they run amok in his mind, he experiences neither pent-up frustration nor sexual impotence. His fantasies and feelings have free play without his being fixated on any one of them. He dispels Mara's daughters as effortlessly as does "the wind a fallen cotton tuft."

Nowhere is Mara's treachery more apparent than when he suggests that death is nothing to worry about. For while personifying death, Mara is that quiet, consoling conviction that one will be exempt from it. "Long is the life span of human beings," he whispers. "One should live like a milk-sucking baby." Mara infantilizes us, makes us crave the blissful forgetfulness of being cuddled and nourished. He jump-starts the furious insistence to have what we want and the whine of thwarted desire. "Short is the life span of human beings," counters Buddha. "One should live as if one's head is on fire."

Mara is the existential trickster. His ambiguity and unpredictability reflect the ambiguity and unpredictability of life itself. Not only does he appear in a bewildering variety of forms, his moods lurch from arrogance to despair. He can speak with detached reason one moment, only to hurl insults and taunts the next. Like the forces of nature, he is consistently unpredictable. We cannot foresee what Mara will do next, but we can learn to recognize his signature.

In order to "read" Mara, Buddhism developed a theory of four maras:

- the devil of psychophysical existence
- the devil of compulsions
- the devil of death
- the devil who is born of a god

This classification disentangles Mara's key features: Mara permeates our physical, emotional, and mental life; he animates the compulsive anxieties and fixations that besiege us; he hovers around us as the imminence of death; he breaks into our lives like a capricious and powerful god. Another mara is sometimes added: the devil of conditioning. This is our biological, social, and psychological history—the drives, conventions, patterns, and habits that urge us to follow the most familiar course of action irrespective of how inappropriate or destructive it might be.

Yet, no matter how carefully Mara is analyzed and classified, the devil eludes precise definition. By trying to define him, one risks losing sight of him. He slips through the bars of the cage in which one seeks to contain him. His polymorphous perversity is most effectively communicated by representing him figuratively. For a personality alone can contain the puzzle of his awkward multiplicity. In the end, we humans are the only adequate metaphor for the devil.

Words and concepts are indispensable in order to make sense, but there is something devilish about the way we think and speak. Mara's snares seem built into the structure of language itself. "A *picture* held us captive," reflected Wittgenstein. "And we could not get outside it, for it lay in our language, and language seemed to repeat it to us inexorably." By abstracting and isolating something from the complex web of relations in which it exists, concepts enable us to develop illuminating and useful theories about it. But they can also trick us into assuming that their definitions are somehow etched into the fabric of life itself. Having defined my sense of self by enclosing it within a picture, I am liable to assume that "I" am as neatly segregated from the world as the picture's outline suggests. Rather than helping me see how I am contingent on a multitude of shifting conditions, the concept of self tends to reinforce my sense of being necessary and apart.

In hardening the difference between Buddha and Mara in

order to define them, concepts obscure their symbiotic relationship. Isolating Buddha's shadow in the person of Mara may have served well as a literary and didactic device, but it allowed the possibility of the two figures becoming further split apart. Over the centuries, this culminated in Buddha's becoming impossibly perfect and good and Mara's being marginalized as a mere caricature of evil. Yet what seems evident from the exchanges between Buddha and Mara in the early discourses is how awakening, freedom, and sanity are only intelligible in the context of confusion, constriction, violence, and chaos.

Mara is Buddha's devilish twin. Buddha needs to let go of Mara in order to be Buddha. And not just once as an episode in the heroic drama of enlightenment. As long as Buddha lives, he is constantly relinquishing Mara. For Mara is the self to Buddha's selflessness, the fear to Buddha's fearlessness, the death to Buddha's deathlessness. The two are inseparable. Buddha has "become invisible" to Mara, yet Mara still stalks him. Mara addresses Buddha as though he were a stranger, but he is really Gotama's own conflicted humanity.

4

Satan—The Adversary

AS MARA SCRAMBLES to gain a foothold on those who seek to free themselves from his grip, he assumes any tactic to suit his purposes. The figure who tempts Christ in the wilderness plays the same wily game as does Mara against Buddha. While Satan tempts Jesus to "command this stone that it be made bread," Mara suggests to Gotama that "he need only resolve that the Himalaya . . . should become gold, and it would become gold." While Satan promises Christ dominion over all the lands of the world if only he will worship him, Mara entreats Buddha to "exercise rulership righteously: without killing and without instigating others to kill, without confiscating and without instigating others to confiscate, without sorrowing and without instigating others to cause sorrow."

In the figure of Mara, Buddhism finds common ground with the monotheistic traditions of the Near East and parts company with the indigenous traditions of India. Except in Buddhist texts, the struggle between good and evil in Indian thought is never consolidated into two polarized figures such as Buddha and Mara. Instead, the powers of evil, death, and destruction are distributed among a number of gods: Yama, lord of death; Kamadeva, god of desire; Shiva, destroyer of the world; Kali, devouring mother; Krishna, divine trickster. Although Buddhists occasionally identified Mara with some of these figures, nowhere does Mara himself appear in Hindu mythology.

The Buddhist and Abrahamic traditions followed a trend that started with Zarathustra, founder of the ancient Zoroastrian religion, which originated between 1000 and 600 BCE in Persia and spread both east and west. Zarathustra taught how Ohrmazd (God) gave birth to twins. While one twin chose to follow truth, the other—Ahriman (the devil)—chose to follow lies. Zoroastrian texts describe Ahriman as "the Destroyer . . . the accursed destructive spirit who is all wickedness and full of death, a liar and a deceiver." Ahriman's opposition to Ohrmazd is the reason human existence is rooted in a primordial tension between the opposing forces of light and darkness, good and evil. In *Ecce Homo,* Nietzsche wrote, "Zarathustra was the first to see in the struggle between good and evil the actual wheel in the working of things."

Whether or not they were influenced by Zoroastrian ideas, the figures of Mara and Satan suggest how Buddhism and the monotheistic faiths grasped the crisis of the individual human self in a broadly similar way. Zarathustra may simply have been the first person to articulate the dilemma of a newly emerging sense of self. As increasingly self-aware and autonomous persons evolved, humans found themselves struggling to cope with the unacceptable drives and desires that besieged them from within as well as the ever-present destructive potential of the natural world and other people. The price of becoming self-conscious was an acutely enhanced awareness of internal and external powers that threaten to overwhelm and destroy one. Since coming to terms with such a self entails confronting its diabolic nature, Buddhism and the monotheistic religions can be understood as different ways of living with the devil.

Buddhist emphasis on the doctrines of "no-self" and "emptiness" has obscured the extent to which Buddha acknowledged and encouraged the emergence of such selfhood. Gotama's critique of caste was a call for each person no longer to define him- or herself in terms of their birth but in terms of what they do with their lives. "No one is *born* a brahmin," he said. "A brahmin is a brahmin because of what he *does.*" For the first time in Indian religious literature, the events around Buddha take place in an historic rather than a mythic setting. This is a world where the gods have been deposed and marginalized, leaving fallible humans to confront the tasks of ordering society and finding salvation through their own efforts.

The Book of Job (composed around 550 BCE, the time of Buddha's birth) offers a glimpse into a similar world where an ordinary man who is neither a prophet nor a king struggles to understand his own fate. The text tells of how one day the sons of God came to present themselves to Him. Among them was Satan. Asked by God whence he came, Satan said: "From going to and fro in the earth, and from walking up and down in it." In the Old Testament, Satan is a function and emissary of God rather than a personification of evil. God is conscious of how Satan moves him needlessly to destroy the "perfect and upright" Job. "Put forth thine hand now," suggests Satan, "and touch his bone and his flesh, and he will curse thee to thy face." Dispatched by God to tempt this paragon of integrity, Satan "smote Job with sore boils from the sole of his foot unto his crown."

Job's tormented account of human life as inexplicably, inescapably, and unpredictably painful evokes the sense of Mara as permeating the very stuff of psychophysical existence. Job likewise is besieged by his devilish God: "His troops come together," he says, "and raise up their way against me, and encamp round about my tabernacle." No matter whether we understand the driving force of creation as God, gods, karma, or biochemical reactions, it seems to relish waging war against us. At times life itself seems to militate against the fulfillment of our longings. Job cries in despair: "*Why is light given* to a man whose way is hid, and whom God hath hedged in?" At times there appears no way out of Mara's snare.

Both Buddha and Christ are described as "victors" over the devil. After his awakening, Buddha is called a "Mara Conquering Sage," while through his death Christ destroys "him that hath the power of death, that is, the devil." The Buddhist nirvana is likewise called the "deathless." Though embedded in different cultural traditions, Gotama's struggle with Mara and Jesus' with Satan point to a common awareness that to be fully human entails coming to terms with a diabolical power that seems to stand in the way of our realizing meaning, truth, and freedom.

In the mythic worldviews of both traditions, the devil is portrayed as a god who rules the world. In Buddhism, Mara is identified with Kamadeva, the Indian god of desire, who has dominion over the entire sensual realm inhabited by animals, men, and the lesser gods. As Kamadeva, Mara shares in the majesty and luminosity of these gods, which is reflected in his haughtiness. "You are a human being," says Mara to Buddha,

> whereas I am a god. You will not escape me. Your body
> is born of a mother and father, a heap of boiled rice and
> sour milk . . . ; while my body is made of mind.

The Koran likewise tells of how, when God created Adam, he commanded the angels to bow down before his new creation. Satan alone refused. "I am nobler than he," he says to God. "You created me from fire, but you created him from clay." As a result of his pride, he is banished by God from heaven but then reprieved until the day of resurrection. "Lord," says Satan, "since You have seduced me, I will tempt mankind on earth." He then proceeds to "cunningly seduce" Adam and Eve in paradise.

John's gospel describes the devil as the "ruler of this world." In his second letter to the Corinthians, Paul calls Satan "the god [*theos*] of this age [*aion*]." He spells out the implications to his followers in Ephesus:

> We are not contending against flesh and blood, but against the principalities, against the powers, against the world rulers of the present darkness, against spiritual hosts of wickedness in heavenly places.

This rich metaphorical language is a way of talking about all the despotic and pervasive forces that constrain our lives. We can understand the devil as those intimidating fiscal, social, political, and religious powers, which we reify into such entities as the Economy, Society, the Government, or the Church, and then treat as though they possessed a personal agency that has the power to condemn or destroy us.

"For the demonic," reflects the theologian Paul Tillich, "is the elevation of something conditional to unconditional significance." Each time something contingent and impermanent is raised to the status of something necessary and permanent, a devil is created. Whether it be an ego, a nation-state, or a religious belief, the result is the same. This distortion severs such things from their embeddedness in the complexities, fluidities, and ambiguities of the world and makes them appear as simple, fixed, and unambiguous entities with the power to condemn or save us. Far from being consciously chosen by individuals, such perceptions seem wired into the structure of our psychological, social, religious, and biological makeup.

In their own ways, Buddhism and Christianity affirm the extraordinary power and extent of the devil's reach. Christ's victory over Satan is all the more moving when understood as the overthrowing of these "principalities and powers" in their totality. In completely surrendering himself with love to the potent and destructive contingencies of his historical existence, Jesus breaks with the demonic and heralds the possibility of a radically new way of being. In accepting his destiny, he knows that he "must suffer many things, and be rejected of the elders and of the chief priests, and scribes, and be killed and after three days rise again." When Peter tries to dissuade him from this course, he says, "Get behind me, Satan."

Far from being God's agent, as he was for Job, by the time of the New Testament, Satan has become a fallen angel. The Book of Revelation describes how "that old serpent, called the Devil, and Satan, which deceiveth the whole world" has been cast out of heaven to rule hell. Jesus himself declares that he "saw Satan fall like lightning from heaven." As Kamadeva, a long-lived but nonetheless mortal god, Mara too will descend to lower realms on account of his evil acts. Such was the fate of a previous Mara, called Dusin, who "fell bodily into the great hell of Avici." Another myth, reported by the eleventh-century Tibetan Gampopa, tells of how Mara already "dwells five hundred miles below this earth" in the form of Yama, the lord of death.

In John Milton's seventeenth century epic poem *Paradise Lost,* Satan is presented as the rebel angel who mounts an insurrection against God because he cannot tolerate the idea of being subordinate to Christ. At the root of his rebellion lies the conceit that he is eternal: "We know no time," he declares to his fellow gods, "when we were not as now." Instead of being created and contingent, he is convinced they are necessary and autonomous: "self-begot, self-raised / By our own quick-'ning power." As the rebellion gains force, his head bursts into flame and from its left side his daughter Sin is born. Satan falls in love with his "perfect image," and their incestuous union produces a son called Death, who then rapes his mother to beget a host of "yelling Monsters." Driven out of heaven by Christ, Satan is banished to hell, where he vows to corrupt humanity, God's new creation.

The devil assumes the form of the serpent who tricks Eve into eating the forbidden fruit by persuading her that it will transform her into a god just as it elevated him into an articulate snake. Out of sympathy for Eve, Adam tastes the intoxicating fruit so that both "swim in mirth, and fancy that they feel / Divinity within them breeding wings." But the self-indulgent ecstasy wears off, and they recognize the tragic condition into which they have fallen.

They sat them down to weep, nor only Tears
Rain'd at their Eyes, but high Winds worse within
Began to rise, high Passions, Anger, Hate,
Mistrust, Suspicion, Discord, and shook sore
Their inward state of Mind, calm Region once
And full of Peace, now tost and turbulent.

Satan is in perpetual rebellion against God; Mara is in cease-less struggle with Buddha. The psychological root of this rebellion is the conceit of being a static self, severed from all relationship, that renders intolerable the notion that we might be contingent on anything but our own innate power. This alienation engenders restlessness and strife, in which we lurch from arrogance to despair. Just as Milton's Satan generates his daughter Sin, so Mara fathers his daughters Craving, Discontent, and Lust. And just as Satan and his daughter gave birth to Death, so Mara and his daughters drive the cycle of existence that repeatedly hurls us into birth only for Yama to cut us down at death.

The devil is the contradictoriness of our nature. As soon as we make a foolhardy commitment to "enlightenment" or "salvation," we start being torn apart by diabolic forces we only dimly understand and can scarcely control. For when we choose to follow a path that Buddha described as "going against the stream," we choose to confront those fears and desires that hitherto we had either repressed or acted out. Like someone who has been swimming downstream with minimal effort only to discover how exhausting, uncomfortable, and unrewarding it is to swim against the current, so one who embarks on such a path will invariably encounter a legion of obstacles.

The devil extends from that inner enemy who voices our most private doubts, conceits, and loathings to that outer enemy who afflicts us with disease, terrorizes us with real and imagined dangers, and ultimately kills us. Each time we feel ourselves slipping into temptation or paralyzed by the collapse of the stock market, we notice the devil at play. But the devil is never alone. For just as there can be no shadow without a body to cast it, there can be no devil without a buddha (an awake one) to know him. The destruction of "this last enemy," writes the Church father Origen of Alexandria, "will not be its nonexistence, but its ceasing to be an enemy and death."

5

Boredom and Violence

CHARLES BAUDELAIRE's genius was to recast the Christian myth of the devil in the light of the emerging plight of an alienated and skeptical human consciousness. While mourning the end of the classical age that had nurtured Dante and Milton, Baudelaire anticipated with resignation a modernity that was crystallizing in his own person. He understood the devil as an intrusive, unsettling presence in the heart of a secular, introverted culture. Among the "yapping, yelling, groaning, creeping monsters," he detects "one more ugly still, more evil, more foul!"

> *Who makes no grand gestures or cries,*
> *He would happily wreck the earth*
> *And swallow the world in a yawn.*

"It's Boredom [*l'Ennui*]!" he declares, "that sensitive monster," a compound of frustration and annoyance that switches between maudlin self-pity and distracted reverie. This is a modern variant of what Buddha called *dukkha:* the fearful anguish knit into our mortal condition.

Baudelaire's collection of poems *Les Fleurs du Mal* (*Flowers of Evil,* 1857) struck that keynote of contemporary anguish which haunts much of the literature and philosophy written since. In Kafka and Beckett, Kierkegaard and Sartre, we find the same brooding disquiet. Baudelaire's poems are the first steps on the path that leads to the splintered nihilism of *The Waste Land* and *American Psycho.*

The mid-nineteenth-century concept of evil still carried echoes of the theological distinction between "natural" and "moral" evil. "Natural evil" referred to all the ills and catastrophes that befell you in life, while "moral evil" denoted the thoughts, words, and deeds associated with sin, suffering, and death. At the beginning of the twenty-first century, a sense of natural evil has all but been lost. To describe diseases or floods as "evils" sounds strained and archaic. Even in its moral sense, "evil" has mutated into a term of moralistic revulsion, used to condemn those who commit acts we abhor. Baudelaire speaks with such clarity because his verses illuminate that modern conception of evil as a failing of the self rather than a feature of reality itself.

"Stupidity, error, avarice, sin," he says, "engage our minds and work our bodies." Evil urges prompt us darkly and furtively from the obscure depths of our self. For Satan lies beside us at night, resting his head "on the pillow of evil." We think of ourselves as free and independent agents, but Baudelaire insists that the devil "has long cradled our enchanted mind. And the rich metal of our will / Is vaporized by this savant chemist." "The Devil pulls the strings that stir us!" he says. "Tight and teeming like a million parasites, / A populace of Demons cavorts in our brain." The theological concepts of "the devil" and "demons" have taken a psychological turn. They are ciphers for something sinister and troubling within us that we dimly intuit but do not understand.

An impersonal sense of evil nonetheless persists. In his poem "Destruction," Baudelaire writes:

> *Ceaselessly the Demon races at my side;*
> *He swims around me as an impalpable breeze;*
> *Which I inhale—I feel it burn my lungs*
> *And fill them with eternally guilty desire.*

The poet suspects that the source of this disturbing but irresistible feeling is something dynamic but insubstantial existing apart from himself ("an impalpable breeze"), over which he has no control but which he cannot help breathing. Although "guilty desire" seems irredeemably "mine," I do not choose to feel such an emotion. It happens to me, breaks into consciousness, *as though* it came from elsewhere. Being prone to such random attacks on the privacy of my soul, I become subject to the destructive potential of the demonic. "When we breathe," says Baudelaire, "Death's invisible river / Pours into our lungs with faint moans." In capitalizing "Death," Baudelaire links it to "Devil" and "Demon," recalling the theological identification of death with Satan and anticipating the Freudian struggle between *eros* (desire) and *thanatos* (death).

The European Enlightenment of the seventeenth century inaugurated a period in which the demonic lost its identity, leaving us unsure of what, if anything, it stands for. The soul of early modern man found itself split in two: detached Cartesian reason at odds with exuberant Wordsworthian emotion. Since the rationalists believed in systematic human progress and the establishment of an ordered world, they demonized chaotic outbursts of unbridled emotion that threatened their goals. The romantics, however, asserted the primacy of feeling and regarded any attempt to impose abstract rules, controls, or measurements onto the spontaneous fluidity of life as a form of demonic inhibition. Nietzsche regarded the moribund state of European civilization as the legacy of a stifling Apollonian tradition of repression that needed to be revitalized by a resurgence of Dionysian energy and passion.

Over the past hundred years, management of this conflict within individual human minds has largely fallen to psychologists and psychotherapists. Freud understood our anxious sense of self (ego) to be forged by two opposed and irreconcilable forces: the blind drives of biology (the largely unconscious id) and the moral constraints of society (the superego).

Both these forces are characteristic of Mara: the tempestuous longings and fears that assail us, as well as the views and opinions that confine us. Whether we talk of succumbing to irresistible urges and addictions or being paralyzed by neurotic obsessions, both are psychological ways of articulating our current cohabitation with the devil.

By identifying boredom as a primary evil, Baudelaire understands the demonic more as oppression and inhibition than as violent or erotic abandon. For when we do transgress, we do so guiltily. "We steal a secret pleasure on the side," he says, "That we squeeze hard like an old orange." This disturbing awareness of being psychologically and morally ensnared by forces we scarcely comprehend reappears in the novels of Franz Kafka. "Someone must have been telling lies about Joseph K.," opens *The Trial,* "for without having done anything wrong he was arrested one fine morning." Poor K. never finds out why he was arrested, fails to penetrate very far into the labyrinth of the judicial system, and finally is executed. The devil as "a liar" and "a murderer from the beginning" who blocks our path (*arrests* us) has assumed the guise of sinister, invisible powers that without apparent reason invade and destroy an ordinary person's life. This acutely secular entrapment is captured by the spare, halting prose of Samuel Beckett: "Suddenly, no, at last, long last, I couldn't anymore, I couldn't go on. Someone said, You can't stay here. I couldn't stay there and I couldn't go on."

In confronting the demonic with little prospect of redemp-

tion, these writers practice a curiously civilized kind of nihilism. While appearing to shun any hope of religious salvation,
they achieve, at least momentarily, a secular salvation in the
transformative workings of their art. Their despair is redeemed
by becoming a beautiful despair. Baudelaire admits as much in
one of his projected prefaces to *Les Fleurs du Mal:* "It seemed to
me pleasant, and all the more agreeable as the task was difficult, to extract the *beauty* of Evil" (Baudelaire's italics). The
poet enjoys an aesthetic pleasure in the very act of coming to
terms with the demons that torment him. Just as knowing
Mara frees Buddha from Mara's grip, reimagining the devil
loosens the bonds with which the demonic binds the poet. The
stifling desperation evoked in the poems contrasts with the effortless and fluid rhythms of each verse. Describing his plight
at the hands of the Demon, Baudelaire seems to be borne away
on the "impalpable breeze" that envelops him:

> *So he leads me, far from God's sight,*
> *Gasping and broken with fatigue, in the midst*
> *Of Boredom's profound deserted plains*
>
> *And throws in my bewildered eyes*
> *Soiled clothes, open wounds*
> *And the bleeding apparatus of Destruction.*

This "apparatus of Destruction" is the systemic violence that
permeates and infects the totality of contingent events. For

created things are subject to breakdown, corruption, deception, and extinction. They are ultimately unreliable. No matter how well we care for this organism of flesh and nerves and blood, it will one day fail us. "The undependable lord of death," remarks Shantideva, "waits not for things to be done or undone. Whether sick or healthy, this fleeting life cannot be trusted." The stuff of which we are made, that allows the possibility of consciousness, love, and freedom, will also destroy us, wiping out that poignant identity of a sensitive creature with an unrepeatable history, who has become a question for itself.

Disease, ageing, and death are forms of an internal violence that afflicts all creatures; whereas natural disasters, viral infections, and terrorist attacks are examples of an external violence that threatens to break out anywhere. The globalized, interconnected world has become a body that is prone to these outbursts without warning. In a way that Baudelaire could not have imagined, we are capable of feeling the instability and vulnerability of the living system of which we are a part and on which we depend. Whether it be the appearance of a virus, a hole in the ozone layer, or a hijacked plane, such events are rapidly and vividly made known through the electronic media. They do not have to impinge on our personal existence or occur very often to frighten us. Mara's most effective weapon is sustaining a climate of fear.

Cancer cells and suicide bombers share the capacity to occupy the space of one's body without one's consent. Every act of violence is a violation of the integrity of my enfleshed being. Whether it be a breaching of my skin, my immune system, or my right under law to live unmolested, a violent act is an intrusion into the intimate space I cherish as my own. Whoever or whatever deprives me of the right to that space violates me. That violence is a form of rape is implied by the French *le viol* (rape) and *violer* (to rape). Whenever humans resort to violence, men are murdered and women raped. That inviolable space they regard as their own is penetrated against their will by a bullet or a penis.

Acts of genocide, child abuse, and terrorism are perpetrated by educated, civilized, and religious people. The willingness to violate others furtively behind closed doors or defiantly in the name of a higher good (the survival of a nation or the truth of a religion) is readily concealed behind a smiling or pious exterior. When these evildoers are exposed, the world heaps scorn and hatred upon them, apparently unaware of the violent impulses from which its own reactions stem.

"It is more difficult to love God than to believe in him," said Baudelaire elsewhere in his abandoned preface.

> By contrast, it is more difficult for people of this century
> to believe in the devil than to love him. Everybody serves
> him, but no one believes in him. The sublime subtlety of
> the devil.

I may sincerely believe in doing good and renouncing evil, but my thoughts and actions often suggest that I wholeheartedly do neither. In the quiet and lonely solitude of the soul, inadmissible urges co-exist with yearnings to act justly and kindly. Both exert an equal claim on my attention. I oscillate between them, one moment consumed with self-loathing only in the next to be granted access to a rapture of compassion. It is here, in the heart of this inner space, that we first face the challenge of living with the devil.

Two

Creating a Path

6

Fear and Trembling

"ALL THE UNHAPPINESS of men," remarked Pascal, "comes from one thing: not knowing how to stay quietly in a room." Sitting still on your own confronts you with the intolerable contingency of your existence. You feel the breath come and go, the heart thud, a jab of pain in the lower back, a ringing in the ear, another anxious cascade of thoughts. When Michel de Montaigne retired to his country estate in 1571, he hoped to leave his mind "in complete idleness to commune with itself, to come to rest, and to grow settled." To his surprise it turned out to be "like a runaway horse" confronting him with "chimeras and imaginary monsters, one after another, without order or plan."

To be thrown into existence is painful and shocking. I was forced from my mother's uterus to emerge bloodied and screaming, gasping for air in an alien world. I had no choice in the matter. As I learned to organize the chaos of the senses into an intelligible world, negotiate the labyrinth of language and signs, get used to hearing and telling my own and others' stories, I discovered that I would be expelled from the world's stage as unceremoniously as I was thrust upon it.

Rather than face the contingency of my existence, I flee it. This existential flight is the diabolic undercurrent of human life. It is that bewildered and fearful recoil against having been born and having to die, that brooding anxiety that is not anxious about anything in particular. Its quivering unease is like the lazy collision of two rings of ripples on water: one a reverberation from the shock of birth, the other an intimation of the shock of death.

I am divided against myself. Part of me remains aware of how weird it is to be this self-conscious animal; another part averts its gaze and flees to the security of what seems manageable. I succumb to an insatiable fascination with trivia and gossip. I crave stimulation and intoxication. I suffer an uncontrollable tendency to daydream, a chronic inability to remain focused on what matters most. In spite of lofty aspirations to pursue a path, I begin to suspect that I am spinning in circles.

The relative constancy of the "I" is exaggerated into a permanent and disconnected self that seems to protect me against the terror of contingency and change. I feel as though I am an unborn, immortal soul temporarily inhabiting a body. To believe in this only intensifies the contradictions of existential flight. For this seemingly eternal self is afflicted with a gnawing doubt that something essential to it is lacking. I appear to be self-sufficient, but crave to be loved and recognized by others; I project self-assurance, but feel as though I'm wearing a mask; I present a cheerful exterior, but inwardly suffer a quiet desperation; I affirm my singularity, but suspect that I am a jumbled collection of roles.

Existential flight is driven by fear. One of the armies of Mara, fear penetrates deep into the roots of human existence. It originates in the very feeling of being contingent: that deep, intuitive anxiety that one need not have been born and will inevitably die. This diffuse anxiety manifests as my concrete fear of rejection, of failure, of cancer, of madness, of senility. Such anxiety and fear seem to brood beneath the surface of awareness, waiting to rise up and seize me. One moment I am contentedly going about my business, only in the next to find myself gripped by an irrational dread. Fear darkens and paralyzes the mind, transforming a world of enticing possibilities into one of malicious indifference toward me. Fear unnerves me, making me panic and act rashly. When fear rules, I become neurotically convinced that something awful is about to happen.

This body that thrills to the prospect of pleasure recoils at the hint of pain. From the cries of the newborn infant to the complaints of arthritic old age, the organism struggles to be free from the suffering knit into its condition. With each footstep, we run the risk of tripping and falling, bumping into an obstacle, inadvertently slipping a disc or pulling a muscle.

Every worry reveals a preoccupation with not getting hurt. Every plan for the future is an attempt to eradicate the anxiety that gnaws on the margins of the present.

Fear is the longing not to be hurt; the craving not to suffer misfortune; the yearning not to be contingent. It is the fundamental aversive reaction to the threats with which life confronts us. As well as being an emotion in its own right, fear pervades all self-centered emotion. Whether I am consumed by hatred or riddled with doubts, in both cases I am afraid— I want to avoid the pain inflicted by an enemy's barbed remarks as much as I do the anguish of my own uncertainty.

As he approached the final rupture with those powers that had hitherto dictated the terms of his life, Gotama unleashed deeply latent fears. "Mara conjured up his host," relates the Sanskrit *Mahavastu,* "and advanced to the bodhisattva's seat. Mounting his chariot drawn by thousands of horses and carrying a dazzling bow, he uttered a fearful cry: 'Kill him, kill him, seize him, quick!'" At his command, hordes of animal-headed demons surged around Gotama, large-bellied snakes crawled out of the earth, goblins rained down embers upon him. The very intensity of his quest for freedom provoked equally intense fright. "The less the sage feared the frightful hosts of that multitude," says Ashvaghosa in his second-century-CE account of Buddha's life, "the more did Mara continue his attacks in grief and anger."

When Pascal said, "The eternal silence of these infinite spaces frightens me," he expressed a longing not to be hurt that goes beyond being afraid of a particular object or person. Pascal's dread came from his awareness of being enclosed in a vast and indifferent universe from which he would soon be expelled. Such fear is the anxiety we feel when the transitoriness and contingency of our existence become apparent. But as well as feeling anxious, we might also feel awestruck. Although this anxiety might undermine a sense of being a separate self, it reveals something infinitely fascinating and terrifying. Some would consider this revelation as religious in nature. It is an intimation of the sublime power that creates, sustains, and destroys all life, before which one feels humbled.

Although recoiling in fear from life's destructiveness triggers Mara's instinctive strategies of closure, it also allows a glimpse of what we need to understand and tolerate if we are to be free from Mara's control. Buddha's victory over the forces of Mara is a way of describing how he has come to terms not only with the limiting and distorting powers in his own mind but also with the powers of contingency and change that drive the world itself. In relinquishing the obsession of being an isolated self, Buddha opens himself fearlessly and calmly to the tumult of the sublime.

In a theistic context, to be afraid of the devil is not the same as fearing God. In the former case, one is terrified of something unpleasant happening to oneself, whereas in the latter, one is awestruck by the terrible power and mystery of what transcends one. When Paul in his letter to the Philippians urged his followers in his absence to "work out your own salvation with fear and trembling," he was inciting them to live their lives in constant awareness of their finitude and mortality. By facing what is limitless and unbounded, such fear cannot be equated with the limiting and constricting fear that belongs to Mara. Instead of driving us round and round in a futile quest for that perfect situation where all pain is banished, this fear opens up a path that might free us from fear.

For Tsong-kha-pa, writing in Tibet at the end of the fourteenth century, fear is one of the causes that brings one to the path opened up by Buddha. This fear too is not one of Mara's "troops." It is fear of Mara himself. This longing not to be hurt by the armies of Mara is the beginning of faith: a yearning to transcend one's limitations and embark on a path. Lacking this wider perspective, we try to ward off fear by desperately avoiding or destroying whatever seems to pose a threat to our well-being. We are unlikely to notice that the strategy itself may be flawed. For no matter how many heads you cut off this Hydra-like Mara, another will grow in its place. Only by stepping back to contemplate this broader picture do you start to realize what is truly frightening: being trapped in a cycle of fearful reactivity.

Even after their awakening, Mara approaches Buddha and his followers "in order to arouse fear, trepidation and terror" in them. Their ability to remain fearless in the face of Mara's threats is taken as a sign that they are no longer subject to their patterns of reactive behavior. Mara tries to distract the beautiful nun Uppalavanna from her meditation as she stands alone

at the foot of a tree in a forest by voicing fears of being mo-
lested. "Though a hundred thousand rogues just like you might
come here," she replies, "I stir not a hair, I feel no terror; even
alone, Mara, I don't fear you." Since her life is no longer
driven by the compulsive longing not to be hurt, she can de-
clare to him, "I am freed from all bondage, therefore I don't
fear you, friend."

But as long as one is subject to compulsive reactivity, one
avoids such fears by fleeing to consoling thoughts and images
that spin out of control into irresistible fantasies of oneself as
a character in a trite drama that compels repetition. Each re-
telling provides an entranced respite from fear and anxiety,
and allows you to extract ever keener frissons of pleasure
from the story's detail. These fantasies are isolated episodes of
a larger story that cannot be told. Whether it be a tale of sex
or revenge, it culminates at a point of intense satisfaction—
then starts again. You do not go on to imagine how the following day you will face the person you have just seduced or
humiliated.

The fantasy is a solipsistic act without consequence. It is
both an anxious flight from contingency and a fixation on
something that promises permanent satisfaction and security.
Flight and fixation are two aspects of a single process. They reflect the simultaneous turbulence and frigidity of the demonic. Fixation is a compulsion that is driven and sustained by
flight from the intolerable contingency of things. By holding
on tight to an idea, object, or person, I feel momentarily safe

and unafraid. But in the very act of grasping something, fixation distorts it. Tightening attention around what is desired severs it from the matrix of relationships whence it springs, making it appear necessary rather than contingent. And thus do I find myself viscerally trapped in Mara's most insidious snare.

7

The Devil's Circle

A MAN LOST in a desert can trudge for hours through the sands until he sees ahead of him an unmistakable line of footprints leading to the horizon. But his joy on finding a trail turns to despair when he realizes the tracks are his own. Since one limb was a few millimeters longer than the other, or habit or injury inclined him to step fractionally further with one leg, he consistently veered to the right or left. Without a path or landmark to guide him, he traced a vast circle while convinced he was walking in a straight line.

"Samsara" is a Pali/Sanskrit term that describes life's tendency to repeat itself. In Tibetan, it is translated as *'khor ba,* which means "circling." This circling is an endless round of compulsive flight and fixation. In German, "vicious circle" is *Teufelskreis,* a "devil's circle." Like someone lost in a desert, I feel compelled to struggle ahead, unaware that a devil's circle will only bring me back to where I began. Through the years, I return again and again to the same stock obsessions. I flick through the tome of my achievements in the blink of an eye only to feel that nothing has really happened. I am still the anxious and puzzled child who set out on the journey.

A disciple once found the Sufi sage Mullah Nasruddin eating a pile of chili peppers. The mullah was sweating profusely, his face flushed with pain. When asked what he was doing, he replied, "If only I continue a little longer, I am sure I'll find a sweet one." No matter what experience has taught us, we insist on making the same mistakes again and again. "Live like a milk-sucking baby," urges Mara. Tug at the teat of experience long enough, he seems to be saying, and it will deliver more than mere milk.

A devil's circle is addictive. It raises you to dizzy heights of rapture only to bring you crashing down into troughs of despair. Yet I do not hesitate to start the diabolic cycle again. I find it hard to resist the urge to go through the familiar and comforting motions of a habit, even when I know that the end result will be the anxious craving to repeat the experience again. Whether the obsession is food, power, sex, religion, or a drug, the pattern is the same.

The devilish circling of samsara provides an anesthetic against contingency. By keeping to established patterns of thought and behavior, I seem to keep life's disconcerting impermanence and unpredictability at bay. Regarding myself as a self-sufficient unit of habits and routines provides a shield against contingency's disturbing excess. A devil's circle blinds us to those cracks in the world through which we could step out of its orbit onto a path.

The natural world itself inclines toward stable and predictable patterns: the circling of planets round the sun, the recurrence of the seasons, the phases of the moon, the ebb and flow of oceans, the unfurling of a bud into flower, the organization of a colony of bees, the migrations of birds, the beat of the heart, the divisions of a cell, the replication of sequences of DNA. Samsara is not just a psychological process. Its machinations are at work in our chemistry and biology as much as in the repetitive obsessions of our psyche.

"Samsara" is shorthand for the unconscious and conscious strategies employed to cope with the convulsions of contingency. As an inherited survival strategy, the brain creates the impression of being a fixed self in a relatively stable world that can be manipulated to achieve happiness. By means of concepts and language, this seemingly constant self is able to learn from the past and plan for a future in which it will reap the rewards of what it does now. Having guessed how others are likely to behave, it adopts maneuvers to outwit or exploit them. This innate sense of being a self, as well as the cravings involved in getting what it desires and avoiding what it fears, are built into the organism.

"Everything," wrote Spinoza, "endeavors to persevere in its own being." The human organism compulsively clings to the illusion of its own necessity as tenaciously as the roots of a tree

cling to the soil in which they are embedded. Gotama understood how human freedom is opposed by impersonal forces
that mindlessly assert themselves. By appearing to him as a
farmer, Mara assumes the form of one whose life is locked
into the patterns of repetitive seasonal change. In this guise,
the devil is not merely a demonic distortion of consciousness
but the capacity of the natural world to confine, disturb, and
confuse us.

The troops under Mara's control tend to straddle the awkward divide between body and mind: sensual desire, discontent, hunger and thirst, craving, lethargy, fear, and restlessness
cannot be neatly classified as mental or physical states. Lust is
as much a warm rush of blood to the genitals as an emotional
yearning or erotic fantasy; hunger as much a pang in the stomach as a craving for steak; fear as much a constriction in the
throat as the desperate longing not to be hurt. Buddha refused
to be drawn on the question as to whether soul and body were
the same or different. He regarded such speculation as not
conducive to awakening. By paying unprejudiced attention to
the totality of experience, one discovers an unbroken contin-
uum between what one thinks of as "body" and what one
thinks of as "soul." You cannot specify where the pang in the
stomach ends and the yearning for steak begins.

The conviction of being an abiding, conscious self, disassociated from the body out of which it peers onto the world,
is an illusion generated by biology and reinforced by psychological and spiritual longings for a fixed identity. The sense of

things remaining the same under changing conditions may simply be how the world appears to an organism that requires perceptual constancy in order to function optimally. Yet a person's apparent permanence is seized as an objective truth in our futile quest for something that will forever console us. If illusions and deceptions will improve an organism's chances of surviving to pass on its genes, then selection pressures will favor them. The forces of nature are indifferent to the ensuing confusion caused to featherless bipeds in search of truth and meaning.

When the suspicion dawns that I am going round in circles, I realize what it means to have lost my way. I may have set off on a path with the hope of breaking out of a cycle of habits only for it to have imperceptibly slipped into another familiar and comfortable routine. As life's insidious drift toward repetitive patterns, a devil's circle is incompatible with a path that liberates. To embark on a path is to break free from samsara's cyclical orbit. A path leads into unknown territory, whereas a circle goes over the same ground again and again. The enticing avenues that a devil's circle offers are not paths at all.

8

A Devil in the Way

WHEN A DEVIL'S CIRCLE is replaced by a path, a way is opened up in the fabric of existence that may at first seem like a rupture, a fissure, even a collapse or breakdown. What is familiar and secure is abandoned in favor of a seductive but disturbing unknown. For when you proceed along the open space of a path, you encounter the turbulent rush of contingency. Things are not as stable or predictable as they once appeared. The present moment is nothing but the point at which the future vanishes. The not-yet-come hurtles toward you like an endlessly breaking wall of water into which you have no choice but to step.

The devil is what makes you hesitate in taking that step. He gets in your way. He blocks your path. In making you veer aside to retrace the protective curve of a circle, he severs you from that matrix out of which life springs. Existential conflict is rooted in this primary opposition between the devil and a path. The devil hinders us from proceeding along a path that would liberate us from the dilemmas, desires, and fears that entrap us. The path opens up the possibility of a freedom the devil cannot tolerate.

Ashvaghosa recounts how Kamadeva, the Indian god of desire, is styled "Mara—the enemy of freedom." Asked about the nature of devils, the Tibetan yogini Machik said, "A devil is anything that obstructs the achievement of freedom. . . . There is no greater devil than fixation to a self. Until this is cut off, all devils wait with open mouths." Gotama claimed to have awakened to a middle way that "can be known here and now, as a result of which a mindful person releases his hold on the world." Contrasting his way to that of Mara, he said, "The safe and good path that leads to happiness has been reopened by me, the wrong path closed off, the decoy removed, the dummy destroyed."

Not only does the devil block the way to freedom, he tricks one into following paths that appear promising but lead only to frustration and disillusion. This is what happened to Balaam, as told in the Old Testament's Book of Numbers. Summoned by his king but acting against God's will, Balaam "saddled his ass and went with the princes of Moab." To prevent him from following this course, God dispatched a satan who "stood in the way" against Balaam. As with Job, the satan functions as an "angel of the Lord" rather than an embodiment of evil. His role is nonetheless defined by his blocking the path that Balaam is intent on pursuing.

The root *satan* in Hebrew means "to oppose, to plot against." Satan is spoken of as the "adversary." The meaning of the Greek *diabolos* (translated into English as "devil") is "one who throws something across one's path." Job complains that his diabolic God "hath fenced up my way that I cannot pass, and he hath set darkness in my paths." The Acts of the Apostles depicts the early followers of Jesus as practicing not Christianity but what they called "the way," an echo of Jesus' claim to be "the way, the truth and the life." Such a way leads to salvation through removing whatever hinders progress along it. The Koran presents a similar opposition. Having refused to bow before man, Satan tells God how he will find revenge: "I will waylay Your servants as they walk on Your straight path, then spring upon them from the front and from the rear, from their right and from their left."

In the Buddhist and Abrahamic traditions, the path serves as a metaphor of freedom while the devil stands for whatever inhibits that freedom. The Chinese also gave primary importance to the concept of the way (*tao*) but without developing an explicit counterconcept of the devil. They were nonetheless aware of the diabolic possibilities of nature and human society that cause one to lose one's path. "Heaven and earth are ruthless," writes Lao-tzu. "To them the ten thousand things are but as straw dogs." Imposing famine, pestilence, lightning, and earthquakes, the "Lord of Slaughter" (as Lao-tzu calls Heaven) is indifferent to the longings and fears of mortals. Since the sage understands this to be the way (*tao*) of things, he is not unduly disturbed. "If I think well of my life," comments Chuang-tzu, "for the same reason I must think well of my death."

Unlike the sage, ordinary men

> become entangled with everything they meet. Day after day they use their minds in strife. Their little fears are mean and trembly; their great fears are stunned and overwhelming. They bound off like an arrow or a cross-bow pellet, certain that they are the arbiters of right and wrong. They drown in what they do—you cannot make them turn back.

In losing sight of the way things are, one loses sight of one's path in life. One finds oneself "running one's course like a galloping steed." Only an intuitive understanding of the way can free one from this turmoil to live at ease, with the curiously effective detachment of a sage.

The "True Person" of Lao-tzu and Chuang-tzu lives fully in the world without being overwhelmed by its frenzy and muddle. He is impervious to the social pressures bearing down on him. "He can commit an error and not regret it, meet with success and not make a show." At the same time, he "puts himself in the background; but is always to the fore." Lao-tzu compares the way of the sage to water, which "benefits the ten thousand creatures; yet itself does not scramble, but is content with the places that all men disdain." A path allows water to run freely along and gather within it. This flowing, nourishing, and transparent liquid is what Namuci, the drought-demon, refuses to release.

Mara is not so much opposed to Buddha as to the "ancient path traveled by the awakened ones of old" that Gotama discovered and made known to others. Mara knows that even after Gotama's death, the path he taught will still be available to those who wish to follow it. It is the path—not Buddha—that enables one to escape from Mara's snare.

9

An Empty Space

SO UBIQUITOUS IS the image of a way or path that its metaphoric richness is obscured. Imagine a footpath that cuts across a field, passes through a gate into a wood, winds between the undergrowth and trees, emerges onto a heath, climbs out of view toward a distant range of hills. To the mind's eye it seems superimposed on the landscape: a brown line traced on a green background, a passage weaving darkly through a forest. To say it "cuts," "passes," "winds," "emerges," "climbs" is to think of it as something with agency that stands out in its own right. But if you kneel down on the ground and examine it, what do you find? Nothing. The path is just a gap between other things: the human-sized space between the grasses in the field and the trees in the woodland.

As long as a path serves our purpose, we do not notice it. When walking along a trail in the countryside, we attend not to it but to the landscape that opens up around us. Only when we lose our way do we become conscious that it is no longer there beneath our feet. One moment we are strolling along, only in the next to be gripped with anxiety on finding that the path we had taken for granted has vanished. To lose one's way is to lose one's bearings. We stumble about in a panic, retracing our steps, wondering whether we recognized a landmark, terrified that we are lost. When we find the path again, we are grateful not so much for the muddy trail that draws ahead but the assurance of its leading to a destination.

The path is a cipher of meaning and purpose. One's "path in life" is a convenient way of saying what one's existence is *for*. It sums up all that we value and aspire to. It lets us envision our remaining years as a trajectory stretching ahead on which to realize our hopes. It enables us to stay focused on priorities, whereas to have "lost one's way" is to have lost a guiding vision. Just as the sense of following a path imbues life with meaning, so being lost is linked with aimlessness and despair.

To lose my way is not only to lose a sense of direction but also the freedom to move. A path allows me to walk or run at a steady, rhythmic pace. As soon as I lose it, I find myself struggling through undergrowth, climbing over fallen trees, circumventing heaps of rocks. The anxiety of having lost my bearings is compounded by the frustration of being obstructed. I expend a great deal of energy but make little headway. My relief on recovering a path is that of being able to move freely again. For a path is a space where nothing gets in the way.

One tends to think of space in terms of physical extension and location. A body "occupies" or "fills" a space. For there to be "no more space" means that nothing more can be fitted into a room or a vehicle or a document. Outer space is that virtually infinite expanse speckled with galaxies and stars separated by inconceivable distances. "Inner space" suggests a formless expanse of mind in which thoughts, mental images, memories, and fantasies rise and pass away. Space seems to be the relatively permanent place where temporal events happen.

Buddhist philosophers see space differently. They define it as the "absence of resistance." The space in a room is understood as the absence of anything that would prevent one moving around in it. To cross from one side of the room to the other is possible because nothing gets in your way. Rather than being the place where things happen, space is the absence of what prevents things from happening. The space in the room is nothing in itself; it is just the absence of chairs or tables, glass walls or hidden tripwires that would obstruct movement within it. In encountering no such resistance, we are able to move about freely.

This dynamic concept of space also applies to a path. A footpath is a space because it offers no resistance to placing one foot in front of the other. Its space allows one to move without hindrance. Space is thus a metaphor of *freedom*. Instead of seeing a path as a thing on which one walks, imagine it as the space between things that allows one the freedom to walk. If the English language did not condemn us to separate the path from the act of walking, we could speak of such free movement as "pathing" (as in French one can talk of *une cheminement*). But we don't say "he paths"; we say "he walks *on* a path," thereby giving the impression that a path is just a place where acts occur. By contrast, in Sanskrit the noun *pratipad* (path) comes from the same root as the verb *pratipadyate,* which means "he or she paths."

One moment we are "pathing," only in the next to find ourselves "stuck" and "blocked." We may not have lost our sense of purpose and direction, but feel incapable of making any headway. It is as though a barrier has been placed across our path and we can find no way to surmount it. We feel hindered, trapped, frustrated. The more we struggle to be free of the obstacle, the more we seem to bang our head against a wall. It is as though Mara deliberately puts immovable objects in our way to frustrate our aspirations. We find ourselves paralyzed by an obsession or fear, we meet with accidents and calamities, we are debilitated by diseases and the ravages of ageing.

Progress along the Buddhist path to awakening is said to be "obstructed" by the devil of compulsions. A compulsion is any mental or emotional state that, on breaking into consciousness, disturbs and captivates us. Whether inflamed by anger or inflated by pride, we feel ill at ease and hemmed in. A compulsion encloses us within its boundaries. When overwhelmed by depression, not only are we inwardly sunk in despair but whatever we see, hear, and touch is abhorrent.

Shantideva compares compulsions to "bands of thieves" who lie in wait for an opportunity to invade us and "steal the treasures" of our minds. As soon as there is a lapse in self-awareness, a compulsive thought or image is liable to erupt, triggering a torrent of longing or despair that leaves us rattled and bewildered. As creatures of Mara, compulsions act as if they were autonomous forces. We suffer anxiety or panic "attacks" and feel overwhelmed by unwelcome thoughts. We are seized by feelings and images that we cannot seem to shake off.

The depiction of Mara as an autonomous being who argues with Buddha illustrates how such drives feel as though they *happen* to one. I do not choose to be lustful, lethargic, conceited, or deluded; I find myself feeling that way. I do not decide in advance to think a thought; it comes to me as a ready-made phrase. I talk of "my" desires, "my" fears, and "my" doubts as though I somehow owned and controlled them. But when I try to let go of them, I find that it is not so much I who have them, but they who have me.

Compulsions obstruct the path by monopolizing consciousness. The hypnotic fascination they exert prevents us from attending to anything else. We behave like a rabbit dazzled by the headlights of a car. Not only do compulsions make us lose sight of our goal, they inwardly paralyze us. To escape their grip does not entail suppressing them but creating a space in which we are freed to let them go and they are freed to disappear. "As soon as I know the mind is distorted," says Shanti-deva, "I should remain as steady as a log." Without condoning or condemning what is breaking into consciousness, calmly note that an emotionally charged complex of phrases and images has erupted. You do not have to think of it as "me" or "mine." Having arisen of its own accord, it will pass away of its own accord. Given the space to do so, a compulsion frees itself.

Compulsions not only disturb and enclose, they distort. The emotion of hatred is not possible without a perception of the other as hateful. Everything about the person is repellent: the slant of his mouth, the shrug of his shoulders, the tone of his voice, the cut of his suit. Although he has a wife, children, and friends, it is inconceivable that they could love such a man. A compulsive feeling about someone encloses him or her inside a frozen image.

Such compelling perceptions are rooted in the innate conviction that reality is composed of discrete, fixed units designed to attract, repel, or bore us, while the self who is attracted, repelled, or bored is a separate entity standing aloof and independent. This conviction is so embedded in human consciousness that it is hard to imagine how it could ever be completely uprooted. It is where Mara holds us most tightly in his grip. By paying careful, sustained attention to the fluid and contingent nature of things, we can begin to ease ourselves free of his mesmerizing gaze. The emptiness in which Buddha abides is the space wherein that conviction has lost its potency and thereby its ability to obstruct us.

Once revealed for what it is, the world is opened up as tentative and contingent, impossible to pin down as "this" or "that," "me" or "mine." A thing is what it is not because of an irreducible essence that marks it off from other things but because of the complex and singular relationships that enable it to emerge with its own unique character from the matrices of a contingent world. To emerge contingently like this is what it means for a thing or a person to be "empty."

For the second-century-CE Indian philosopher Nagarjuna, such contingency *is* emptiness. And that emptiness *is* the middle way. Thus emptiness is a path. It is that open and unfettered space that frees us to respond from a liberating perspective rather than react from a fixed position. It is the absence of resistance in the heart of life itself that allows the boundless diversity of phenomena to pour forth in creative profusion and abundance.

10

From Home to Homelessness

WHEN I LOSE my way in a strange land, I lose not only my bearings and freedom to move, but also my connection with others. As soon as I realize I am lost, I feel isolated and alone. The path may have been my sole link to humankind. I might not have seen another person for days, but only when the path disappears am I overcome by loneliness. As a gap between things wide enough for people to pass, a path humanizes the landscape. Lights on a distant hill reveal more than a destination; they connect me with those who lit them.

A path is nothing in itself. It is the impression left by the tread of feet of those who went before. The relief of recovering a path is that of being reconnected with others like myself. Not only can I resume an unimpeded journey to its goal, but I have returned to the fold of my kin. A freshly discarded bottle is as reassuring as a signpost or a bridge. For a path is an intersubjective space. Its free and purposive trajectory is created and maintained by those who use it. Leave it for a year or two, and grasses and weeds will reclaim it. As you walk along a path, you are indebted to every man, woman, child, and dog who preceded you. And each time you place a foot on the ground, you maintain the path for those who will follow. In pushing aside a fallen branch, you take responsibility for those who will come later.

The path evokes an early memory of humankind. For we are nomads, refugees, immigrants, wanderers across the surface of this earth. We come from elsewhere. As creatures in constant motion, we are restless, rarely at ease when standing still. We reject one place in favor of another and move on. We flee catastrophes, tyrannies, and wars. Whether in search of food, work, safety, or meaning, we set out on trails left by others or blaze trails of our own. Wherever we leave our mark—be it on a physical or cultural landscape—we allow the possibility of a path to emerge.

Buddha described commitment to the path as "going forth" from home to homelessness. "In a home," he said, "life is stifled in an atmosphere of dust. But life gone forth is open wide." "Going forth" traditionally refers to the renunciation of household life by a monk or nun, but to an unsettled generation, it is simply a reminder of the human condition. "The foxes have holes," said Jesus, "and the birds of the air have nests; but the Son of man hath not where to lay his head." A sentient being on a ball of rock and mud hurtling through space, who is skeptical about the promises of religion, need not aspire to homelessness.

Homelessness strikes us each time we see through the diabolic illusion of the world as a home that provides security and well-being. Every place that offers itself as a final abode will fail to live up to its promise. Either we will find ourselves frustrated and ensnared by it or will be evicted from it at death. To commit oneself to a path is to abandon the consolations of settling down. One accepts a nomadic destiny in the company of those with whom one is bound by this common fate.

"Narrow is the way," says Jesus, "which leadeth unto life, and few there be that find it." But having found the path is no guarantee that I will not lose it. You might once have stumbled across it by chance, only to spend the rest of your life trying to find it again. You were convinced you had discovered a path only to find yourself tracing another circle. Buddha recognized that it was not enough to find the path. One had to *cultivate* it.

The Pali and Sanskrit word for "cultivation" is *bhavana*. The root of *bhavana* is *bhu,* which means "to be." *Bhavana* means "bringing into being" or "allowing into being." To cultivate a path is to bring its free, purposive, and shared space into being. It is a creative task. As in growing a plant, one creates the conditions that allow it to unfold. By preparing the ground, planting seed, providing sunlight and water, we create a golden field of wheat. Something that previously was not there is now abundantly present.

A path is created by clarifying one's aims and removing what gets in the way of their realization. It is carved from commitment and opened up by letting go. It entails both doing something and allowing something to happen. A path is both a task and a gift. In exerting too much control, one inhibits its spontaneous unfolding, whereas just by letting everything be, one loses sight of a guiding vision. The art of creating a path is to do neither too much nor too little.

As Ch'an (Zen) Buddhism evolved in China, the notion of the path became divided along these lines. Those who saw the path primarily as a *task* described it as a gradual series of steps leading to a goal. Those who saw it primarily as a *gift* envisioned it as a sudden and unpredictable eruption of freedom and insight. The "gradual" path is a trajectory that develops over time; the "sudden" path is an open space in which we are freed to act as the spirit moves us. The gradual path is accomplished by commitment and discipline; the sudden path is beyond the reach of training and seems to burst forth without effort. Creating a path is like learning to play a piano. It may require years of discipline to achieve technical mastery of the instrument, but for the music to come alive requires a sensibility and inspiration that cannot be learned.

As we learn to play this complex instrument of bones, flesh, nerves, impulses, thoughts, and feelings, we trace a path that weaves its way like a channel through the landscape of our experience. It is guided by an intuitive yearning for what we value most deeply; its space is the openness we are able to tolerate within our hearts and minds; it is sustained by the networks of friendship that inspire us to keep going. The path follows the contours of our life as one day turns into the next. It is found amidst the most mundane of circumstances as well as the most sublime. Then we lose it as the story we tell ourselves about ourselves veers off onto another track. Then we find it again. And lose it again.

The path is more than just a task and a gift. In linking one with others, it is also a *bond*. The path unfolds not only within the depths of the soul but also through words and deeds in the world. It extends beyond us through the relationships that connect us to others. Our life is our passage through the world we share. Long after we are gone, that path may still be discerned in the traces we left in those we knew and in the things we created and transformed.

The Tibetans translated *bhavana* as *sgom,* which means to "become familiar" with something. To create a path is to become intimate with the space opening up within, around, and before us. This intimacy comes from mindful awareness of what is unfolding in our body, feelings, minds, and worlds from moment to moment. We get used to the taste, the feel, the texture of the path. It ceases to be something to which we self-consciously aspire. When we stray from it, we feel its loss as an act of self-betrayal.

The Buddhist path extends back two and a half thousand years to Gotama, in whose footsteps numerous generations have followed. It has survived only because people have accomplished its tasks, enjoyed its gifts, and forged its bonds within their lives. If it is to continue into the future, the responsibility lies with those who practice it now. As a shared space, it is contingent on those who tread it. If one generation fails, its fragile openness may be lost.

Yet the well-intentioned urge to preserve a religion runs the risk of mummifying it. Although you might succeed in preserving its institutions and dogmas for a while, you cannot preserve a path any more than you can preserve the current of a river or the whistling of a wind. Insidiously, Mara attempts to secure what by nature is open and fluid. The survival of a path is achieved not by preserving it but by walking it—even when you have no clear idea of where it will lead.

As religions grow from humble beginnings into churches and orthodoxies, the narrow path turns into a brightly lit highway. The risk of embarking on a journey into the unknown is replaced by the confidence of setting off on a well-planned excursion. Homelessness starts to feel like home again. The freedom of the open road is replaced by the drudgery of repeating a cycle of routines. As we proceed along the well-trodden paths of Buddhism, Christianity, Judaism, or Islam, we may begin to weary of their certainties. Perilous trails that branch off the main track and peter out in the anarchy of wilderness catch our attention. We realize that the path we are taking might disappear into a pathless land.

11

What Is This Thing?

AS AN UNIMPEDED SPACE that allows you to go beyond compulsive fixations, a path takes you into unfamiliar territory, where questions begin to outnumber answers, and uncertainty prevails over certainty. The conviction of being a necessary and isolated self is replaced by the perplexity of being a contingent and relational self moving inexorably toward its own end. The path's empty space is animated by a growing awareness of how mysterious and inexplicable it is to be here at all.

Around the turn of the eighth century in China, a young monk called Huai-jang left his monastery on Mount Sung and headed south for Mount Ts'ao-ch'i, a journey of several hundred miles. When he reached Ts'ao-ch'i, he went to Nan-hua Monastery and was introduced to Hui-neng, the sixth patriarch of the Ch'an (Zen) school.

"Where did you come from?" asked Hui-neng.

"Mount Sung," said Huai-jang.

"But what is this thing?" said Hui-neng. "How did it get here?"

Huai-jang was speechless. The exchange of social niceties had turned into something unsettling. Huai-jang remained on Mount Ts'ao-ch'i with this question for the next eight years.

Five hundred years later, in thirteenth century Japan, Zen master Dogen declared Hui-neng's "What is this thing?" to be the nature of Buddha. Since the process of awakening begins with questioning one's existence, one's buddhanature is most adequately expressed as an interrogative. The path opens up as soon as one's life is exposed as a question rather than a bundle of more or less interesting facts. This questioning is not intellectual curiosity. Zen speaks of it being asked through one's skin and bones. It seizes the body and emotions as urgently as it grips the mind. You cannot reflect on it from a comfortable distance. It is inseparable from everything you are.

To question like this is to let go of opinions and remain suspended between all possible answers. Certainties, beliefs, and assumptions are put on hold. One can question only what one does not know. To ask "Where is Mount Ts'ao-ch'i?" is to admit that one knows not where it is. While waiting for the answer, one hovers in the space between all conceivable directions. To ask "What is it that observes the devil at play?" one rests in the strange space of a self-aware creature subject to forces that disturb and enclose it. All possibilities lie open. There are no foregone conclusions. You are momentarily freed from the tyranny of opinion. Mara is deprived of a foothold.

An astonishing thing about life is that it astonishes us. Astonishment quivers at the heart of human consciousness. Can we imagine a future where all questions have been resolved and nothing perplexes us? A time when "what?" and "why?" have lost their meaning? No matter how much knowledge we accrue, at the end of each line of enquiry will there not always be another question awaiting us? One that we cannot foresee until we have answered those that precede it?

To rest in such perplexed astonishment was described by John Keats as "negative capability":

> that is, when a man is capable of being in uncertainties, mysteries and doubts without any irritable reaching after fact or reason.

While Keats understood this quality as the defining trait of the creative artist, it succinctly captures the frame of mind of one who contemplates the question "What is this thing?" When we learn that "irritable" was used in the nineteenth century as a medical term to describe the reflexive nature of a limb to react when subjected to stimulation, its accuracy in describing Zen meditation is heightened. To cultivate astonishment triggers one's habitual craving for the certainties that seem to reside in concrete facts and reasoned conclusions.

Certainties are more consoling than an infinity of questions. To know you are a monk who has just walked all the way from Mount Sung in sandals made of reeds gives you an identity. You feel secure inside the boundaries of that description of yourself. You have no doubts as to who you are. But probe a little deeper—"What are you really? How did *you* get *here?*"—and the boundaries crumble to reveal a mass of unbounded perplexity.

According to legend, when the young man who was to become Buddha left the security of his home to explore the world beyond its walls, he chanced upon a person crippled with age, another ridden with disease, and a corpse. These sights perplexed him. For the first time, his existence became a question for him. The boundaries of his identity collapsed. The certainty of being Siddhattha Gotama—Suddhodana's heir, Yasodhara's husband, and Rahula's father—was an inadequate answer to the question posed by being born and having to die. On returning home he felt trapped. Late one night he slipped away to pursue a path that might lead to a resolution. But Mara was observing this and said to himself, "From now on, as soon as a hint of desire, malice, or cruelty stirs in his mind, I will know it." And so Mara "attached himself to him like a shadow follows the body, waiting for an opportunity."

A path is animated by perplexity and obstructed by fixed ideas. Confusion reigns in its free, purposive, and shared space. We do not know where our questions will lead, but they compel us to seek a response. Yet with each insight we risk being halted in our tracks by the devil. As the imposer of limits and ends, Mara cannot tolerate the limitless and endless nature of astonishment. He is that part of us that is prone to regard any provisional answer as though it were the final word on the matter. When crystallized into an ideology, even the most lucid understanding will trap us rather than free us. "If you meet Buddha," advises the Zen patriarch Lin-chi, "kill him."

The destination of a path depends on the kind of questions that propel one along it. An existential question is presented not only in words but by the wordless astonishment at being alive. Its resolution too is rooted in this dumb surprise. Gotama's existential awakening is already prefigured in the scream of a newborn baby, the anguish of ageing, the humiliation of disease, the decay of a corpse. For only when these things become questions for him can his quest for awakening begin to unfold. His path both originated and culminated in an awareness of the "great matter of birth and death."

Astonishment is a gift. No amount of effort can peel off the stubborn veneer of banality that renders the world flat, routine, and opaque. The mystery that there is anything at all glimmers in the margins of awareness but rarely strikes home in all its intensity. "Because it is so very close, you cannot get this truth out of your eyes," said the twelfth-century Chinese Zen monk Ta-hui. "But if you try to receive it by stirring your mind, you have already missed it by eighteen thousand miles." In spite of Mara's desperate attempts to replace astonishment with a consoling opinion or belief, you only remain true to your quest by allowing the riddle of the world to disclose itself.

12

The Riddle of the World

THE WORDS ON THIS PAGE and the eyes that flit across them originated around fifteen billion years ago when the universe was just an extremely tiny, hot, and energetic drop of space-time. There was no time before and no space outside this drop: all space, all time, and all things were generated from it. As it expanded, it created every quark and lepton, atom and molecule that constitute the estimated hundred billion galaxies in the universe, hundred billion stars in the Milky Way, trillion cells in each human body, and ten trillion synapses in each human brain.

This planet on which our every breath and meal depends coalesced from stardust and interstellar gas into a stable sphere of matter four and a half billion years ago. Within another half-billion years, simple forms of bacterial life had emerged in the oceans. No one yet knows how the first sequences of self-replicating molecules that eventually would generate trilobites, hummingbirds, and chimpanzees arose. Yet alternative theories of creation provide not answers to this puzzle but other questions disguised as answers. To invoke God, mind, or meteor-borne bacteria to explain the origins of life on earth leaves one with equally imponderable questions about God, mind, and meteor-borne bacteria.

A terrestial vertebrate like Huai-jang was only able to walk from Mount Sung to Mount Ts'ao-ch'i because four hundred million years earlier a small group of fish evolved a skeletal structure that would evolve into the kind of spine and limbs that could support the weight of a creature moving on dry land. Driven by adaptive pressures, this evolutionary pathway was selected for reasons peculiar to the subaquatic survival of these fish. Had they been wiped out by a natural calamity or driven to extinction by another fish better suited to that aquatic environment, that pathway would have been cut off and terrestial beings may never have evolved.

When the first mammals appeared on earth, they had to eke out a precarious existence in the crevices and gaps of a world dominated by dinosaurs. Only the sudden mass extinction of these reptiles sixty-five million years ago as the result of an asteroid five miles wide smashing into the Yucatán peninsula allowed the opportunity for mammals and birds to flourish in the vacated ecological niches. Had the asteroid been deflected from its earthbound trajectory by a collision with another chunk of cosmic debris, the evolution of animals whose females suckle their young may never have led to the "improbable and fragile entity" called *Homo sapiens*.

Human beings anatomically identical with ourselves first appeared in Africa about a hundred thousand years ago. For the next ninety millennia these large-brained, tool-making, language-speaking, itinerant creatures subsisted entirely by gathering roots, berries, and plants, scavenging animal remains, and hunting game. Around ten thousand years ago, they learned how to domesticate plants and animals, making possible settled agrarian communities. It took another five thousand years to discover how to extract and use metals. Shortly thereafter, states began to emerge, then writing, cities, and the beginning of history.

The record of the past is inscribed in the background radiation from space, the Doppler shift in light, geological strata of rocks, radioactive decay of carbon, fossils and bones, sequences of genetic code. This scripture of life tells a story in which humans have just appeared as tentative characters in a drama of staggering duration and complexity. Our cherished humanity, which feels to us so necessary, turns out to be contingent upon a bewildering array of unforeseen conditions and chance events. Despite our rapid and pervasive domination of the earth, our violent impact on the biosphere may cause us to disappear from the narrative as abruptly as we entered it.

The universe is indifferent to the fate of sentient beings

who arise and pass away upon the surface of this planet. Millions of species of plants and animals have already become extinct and would have been forgotten had we not unearthed their fossilized remains. Just because life has evolved in such a way to produce beings like us does not mean that we were a foregone conclusion from the outset. According to evolutionary biology, there is no discernible purpose guiding this sublime exfoliation of creatures toward a preordained goal. But once a life-form has emerged through evolution, both its origins and the conditions needed for its survival are intelligible in terms of ordered sequences of causes and effects.

To believe one's existence to be either preordained by the will of God or an inevitable consequence of actions in a former life is consoling because it confirms the deep intuition of one's being necessary rather than contingent. Such views are attractive because of their seeming ability to account for everything that happens to us. It is comforting to be assured that things are the way they are because of remote and mysterious causes that have an intimate bearing on the exigencies of one's particular life. Yet since there is nothing that cannot be explained as the workings of God or the results of karma, these "explanations" explain nothing. Incapable of being either falsified or verified, they have as much explanatory power as a theory that claims life on earth to be under the telepathic control of invisible beings from Alpha Centauri.

The emerging understanding of reality disclosed by the

natural sciences evokes in me feelings of awe incomparably greater than anything religious or mystical writings of any tradition can inspire. Far from being just dumb, inert stuff, matter is wondrously, abundantly, profusely alive. The more we understand it, the less there appears any need for a divine spark or immaterial consciousness to animate it. To accept the wisdom of life's scripture is to accept that we have sprung from the same stuff as carrots and ducks. The fingers that tap these words on a computer keyboard evolved from the fins of a long-forgotten fish, refined their skills through picking lice from fellow monkeys' fur and chipping arrowheads from shards of flint. No matter how perfectly adapted they appear to be for present needs, half a billion years from now they may seem as alien to our remote descendants as are the fishes' fins to us.

Whatever emerges contingently upon a matrix of unstable conditions in turn becomes an unstable condition upon which something else can contingently emerge. We inhabit a universe of relentless motion and flux in which everything from an idle thought to a solar system comes into being then hastens to its end. In the past second, the Milky Way has traveled one hundred and twenty miles closer to the center of its local galaxy cluster, the earth twenty miles in its orbit around the sun, while the brain has generated millions of firing patterns across its neural pathways. In five billion years, the sun is expected to explode, engulfing the earth as it expands beyond the orbit of Jupiter, at which point any sentient life remaining on the planet will become extinct.

While Darwin regarded evolutionary change as proceeding with majestic slowness, meticulous observations of finches on islands in the Galápagos have demonstrated how the birds' beaks are continually being modified in the struggle to adapt to contending environmental forces. The beaks "look solid," concludes the science writer Jonathan Weiner,

> but they are as fluid as ripples on a stream. . . . The closer you look at life, the more rapid and intense the rate of evolutionary change. . . . the farther your remove, the more the living world seems fixed and stable, hardly moving at all.

A similar illusion of solidity and stability is achieved by keeping the awareness of one's own life at a safe existential distance from its contingency and flux. Mara is the part of us that recoils from life's tumult and seeks solace in such illusions, whereas Buddha stands for that capacity to behold, embrace, and transform the turbulent stuff that ceaselessly pours forth.

Each of us is no more necessary or durable in the scheme of things than a shooting star, a piece of cosmic debris burning up as it enters the earth's atmosphere. However much we avert our gaze from the imminence of our demise, we cannot escape the end that Mara holds in store for us. For our death is not an event that will just happen one day: it is etched into the fabric of what we are now. The consciousness of our singularity achieves its bittersweet focus in the intimation of how precarious this life is. As the personification of death, Mara defines us by standing unavoidably in our way. We only feel about ourselves the way we do because we know one day we will vanish.

13

On Being Conscious

EVER SINCE I CAN REMEMBER, this same consciousness has perused colorful shapes with these eyes, listened to
melodies and laments through these ears, handled objects and
caressed bodies with these fingers. This same self has been
worrying about itself and those close to it, replaying the past,
projecting the future, suffering fears, nurturing desires, all in
a fractured monologue uttered silently in the same head.
Thoughts, images, memories, and feelings may come and go,
but the presence of consciousness itself seems irreducible, constant, necessary, and essential—anything but contingent.

Without consciousness, I would lose that most intimate
sense of being who I feel I am. Consciousness enfolds my singularity: the peculiar texture of my inner self that I reach for
but never touch, the tape-loops of thought and feeling that
never will be shared, the snatches of my mother's voice still

calling to the child I was, clips of the past (a door handle, a driveway, a line of ants) that defines me in an indefinable way, the silent mantras of my hopes, secrets, conceits, wounds. And simultaneously, consciousness reveals the public world in which this irreducibly private self feels at home: the blueness of the summer sky, the taste of cumin, Frank Sinatra's voice, the scent of honeysuckle, the rasp of a cat's tongue.

"The fire is at its last click," wrote John Keats late one winter's night in 1819.

> I am sitting with my back to it with one foot rather askew upon the rug and the other with the heel a little elevated from the carpet . . . These are trifles—but . . . Could I see the same thing done of any great Man long since dead it would be a great delight: as to know what position Shakespeare sat when he began "To be or not to be."

Imagine a snapshot of Gotama sitting beneath the bodhi tree, or video footage of Huai-jang walking down the dusty path to Mount Ts'ao-ch'i. The textual record replaces the unrepeatable singularity of these moments with stylized descriptions written down years after the event. Yet we look to these texts not to resolve abstract questions about the nature of existence but specific questions posed by this astonished being-here-now.

A single faded photograph of Buddha would communicate something no amount of exquisite statues and scroll paintings can ever convey. Although the first photograph would not be made until several years after Keats' death, the poet had an intimation of the effect photography would have. For "the Photograph," writes Roland Barthes, "is . . . the sovereign Contingency . . . the *This*." Whereas painting and sculpture seek to represent what is essential and abiding in their subjects, a photograph is a trace of what is fleeting and unrepeatable. "To designate reality," Barthes continues,

> Buddhism says *sunya*, the empty; but better still: *tathata*, the fact of being this, of being thus, of being so. *Tat* in Sanskrit means *that*, which makes one think of the gesture of a small child who designates something with its finger and says: Ta! Da! Ta!

What appears to be most singular about me turns out to be what is most contingent. This identity as a conscious "I," which feels so densely and intractably given, derives its sense of being *this* rather than *that, me* rather than *you*, from the myriad influences, choices, accidents, attributes, and circumstances from which it springs. Each significant step I take in life differentiates me that much more from others. Since each step could have been one that circumstances might have prevented or one I chose not to take, each difference that defines me need not have happened.

That this tentative singularity experiences itself is a mystery. To know what it means to "know oneself" is perplexing.

I am intimately conscious of being conscious, but struggle to find an adequate way to express it. I tend to describe a thing I experience by comparing it to something else I experience. Cumin is compared to fennel, Frank Sinatra to Dean Martin, cats' tongues to sandpaper. But I know no other immediate experience to which *this* immediate experience can be compared. This consciousness that wonders what it is, is the only one to which I have access.

Contemporary neuroscience offers a wealth of evidence to show how consciousness is profoundly connected with the functioning of the brain. A piece of brain "the size of a grain of sand," writes neuroscientist V. S. Ramachandran,

> would contain one hundred thousand neurons, two million axons and one billion synapses, all "talking to" each other. . . . it's been calculated that the number of possible brain states . . . exceeds the number of elementary particles in the universe.

This extraordinarily complex and rapidly firing organ receives constant inputs from the senses, which it converts into a simulation of a world being experienced by a conscious self. Although we feel as though we are peering out of our bodies at the summer sky while caressing a cat, the entire show is a representation generated in the brain. My being conscious of the episode is as much a configuration of neural signals as are the sky and the cat. The picture of a world out there divided from a subject in here, mysteriously connected to each other in the formless ether of "mind," is illusory.

While damage to parts of the brain can radically and predictably alter the nature of consciousness, observation of brain states cannot tell us why or how a particular configuration of neurons is experienced as the last click of a dying fire on a cold winter evening. Nor can it explain how vast arrays of constantly shifting visual, auditory, gustatory, olfactory, tactile, and mental sensations are miraculously unified into the seamless experience of having lunch with an aunt in a bistro in Buenos Aires. Although neuroscience presents a strong case for consciousness being contingent on the brain, it fails to illuminate how the brain generates that crucial and poignant sense of being a self-aware creature in a highly specific, value-laden world.

Buddhism describes consciousness of the summer sky as springing from the impact between a patch of blue color and the unimpaired eyes of an awake organism. As integral parts of the nervous system, the sense organs here take the place of the brain (which is never mentioned in Buddhist studies of mind). Consciousness is not seen as the emergent property of one dominant organ but of an entire system of interconnected processes: external objects, bodily senses, feelings, concepts, language, memories, history. It is not reducible to any one or all of these conditions, nor can it occur without them. Consciousness is the consequence of the interaction between the kind of creature we are and the kind of environment we inhabit.

Human consciousness is ceaselessly affected by a world of which it is aware. To be conscious is always to be conscious *of* something. Whether we are awake or dreaming, consciousness is triggered by images, sounds, smells, tastes, textures, and ideas that constantly bombard us. Even when we turn attention inward to examine consciousness itself, the examining consciousness immediately feels detached from and impacted by the consciousness under examination. For the examining consciousness to be aware of itself is impossible. Just as a finger cannot touch itself and a sword cannot cut itself, so the mind cannot (in this strict sense) know itself.

The world that appears to consciousness comes already colored by tones and shades of emotion. The experience is subjectively registered somewhere along a spectrum whose extremes are ecstasy and agony. Even if an experience is so neutral that we feel indifferent toward it, that indifference is nonetheless a feeling. It can prompt us to act just as efficiently as do feelings of pleasure or pain. When we are bored, we seek stimulation, just as when we pull a muscle we take care not to aggravate the discomfort.

This world of which we are conscious not only feels a certain way, it makes sense to us. It is intelligible. It comes as though preloaded with meanings. You catch a glimpse of a person racing past in a car, and you know without doubt who it is. You read the title of a book, and its meaning jumps out from the letters and words themselves. You do not see dark squiggles on a pale ground that you have to make an effort to interpret. On entering a room for the first time, you are not bewildered by an array of meaningless shapes and colors. You immediately see windows opening up onto landscapes, furniture placed on carpets, paintings arranged on walls.

The world that is given in consciousness is more than a set of sensations and impressions that we receive, feel, and organize. It is an arena of possibilities to be realized through verbal and physical acts. To be conscious is to be on the threshold of responding or reacting to what is unfolding around you. Whether we carefully respond after months of deliberation, or instinctively react without thinking, in both cases we realize what until then was merely a possibility. Even if we decide to do nothing, as a choice that has consequences, that decision is nonetheless an act. We cannot *not* act. We cannot *not* pay attention to the pressures and opportunities with which the world confronts us, even if it is to ignore them.

Buddha regarded consciousness as contingent not only on sensations, feelings, perceptions, concepts, and choices but also on illusions and conditioned behavior. The human organism is instinctively prone to reify the experiencing "I" as a separate conscious entity and to behave as though the world were a domain for gratifying its desires. While modern biology understands this illusion of being an independent and permanent "I" that is always on the verge of finding happiness as an evolutionary strategy conferring survival advantages, Buddha saw how it condemned us to anxiety and frustration.

To assume the way the world instinctively appears to us to be true is to succumb to the trickery of Mara that is built into the structure of the organism itself. As soon as human beings aspired for more than mere physical survival, they found themselves opposed by entrenched habits of perception and behavior that ran counter to the realization of their cultural and spiritual ideals. To undermine the innate impression of being a fixed self in a constant world that promises happiness, Buddha taught his followers to pay sustained attention to the transient, unreliable, and selfless "marks" of existence. He discovered that the key to well-being lies in understanding how this shifting, uncontrollable world is incapable of providing such well-being. Since such practices and insights go directly against Mara's "stream," we find ourselves distracted and obstructed each time we seek to apply them.

As a healer of the human condition, Buddha was interested in consciousness only insofar as that an understanding of its contingency would help free us from the illusions in which it is embedded. For him, the problem with consciousness was the way it appears to be the irreducible core of oneself. Even before we indulge in the religious conceits of being a pure awareness or an eternal soul, consciousness already seems strangely disassociated from the body and world it seems to inhabit. This innate sense of being apart from the flux of life was, for Buddha, one of the root causes of human isolation, alienation, and anguish. In paying mindful attention to how consciousness emerges contingently from fluid conditions, one starts to dissolve the fixed sense of "I" that it seems to enclose. In breaking down the isolation of the alienated self, such awareness reconnects us to the endless play of interacting, mutually creating processes. For Buddha, consciousness, like everything else in the world, was no more stable or real than the flicker of a shadow or the bubbling froth of a brook.

14

This Body Is Breathing

YOU ARE A PARTICIPATING observer of these words. Light from a window or lamp reflects off a line of printed text, generates an image on your retinas, which flashes along optic nerves to neurons in the brain to appear as an intelligible phrase or sentence. Whether the words intrigue, irritate, or bore you, this very experience is where the path to freedom begins. We tend not to see this. For "ordinary men are deluded," remarked the twelfth-century Korean Zen teacher Chinul:

> When donning clothes they only understand that they are donning clothes; when eating they only understand that they are eating; in all their activities they are deceived by appearances. Hence they use the sublime func-

tioning of the mind every day but do not realize it; it is right before their eyes but they are not aware of it.

In taking the everyday details of life for granted, we fail to appreciate the extraordinary fact that we are conscious at all. Like a fish that spends its time swimming through the oceans in search of water, we assume the deepest truths to reside in some transcendent realm beyond the mundane clutter of daily existence. But for Chinul "the sublime essence of nirvana is complete in everyone." In keeping with Zen tradition, he is not proclaiming an abstract truth. Here and now, he insists, Buddha's pristine awareness quivers through the fingers that feel the texture of this book, the eyes that behold these words, the thoughts that puzzle over their meaning.

"The way," said Chuang-tzu, "is in the ant, in the broken tile, in dung, in mire." Nirvana is found not by forsaking the world but by probing its dark and fleshly depths. To break the spell of the body's appearance, imagine making an incision with a scalpel from your forehead to your belly, then peel away the layers of skin, fat, flesh, and sinew until bone is visible. Observe the heart's valves pumping blood through veins and arteries, the stomach processing half-digested food, glistening viscera: liver, kidneys, intestine. How swiftly is that image of oneself, preened in every passing mirror, replaced by revulsion at the human animal.

Those acts of which we are most embarrassed in public— weeping, vomiting, urinating, defecating, copulating—are what least define us as persons. The well-dressed ego struts and displays, but we are ashamed when our common bestiality is exposed to others. This leaking frame is an inescapable reminder of the fragility and impersonality of our condition: its decay, smells, aches, seizures, and breakdowns a cruel mockery of the self-contained personality we struggle to preserve.

"If, possessed of such a body," said Buddha, "one thinks highly of oneself and despises others—that is due to nothing other than a lack of insight." This carnal organism, born from a mother's womb and destined to end as dust, is the great equalizer of beings. Dissect a cat or dog, bird or fish, and beneath the skin you discover flesh, blood, and bones just like your own. That sense of being a cut above the rest is but a shimmering flicker on the surface of the sublime animal that we are. Break down the organic matter further into proteins and genes, and we reach our common heritage with everything from sea grass to bacteria. Analyze the genes into molecules, atoms, and quarks, and we touch what we share with pebbles and comets.

We find ourselves in flight not only from the precariousness of a contingent world but from the demands of an animal's body. We become fixated upon a seemingly eternal self-consciousness, severed from nature, enclosed in a disembodied space. As we read these words, we do not feel the workings of the lungs, heart, and nervous system that make reading possible. The body's delicate tissues and organs are a brute reminder of our mortality. Its need to breathe, eat, and evacuate waste is proof of our embeddedness in nature. Yet to turn attention away from the self's narcissistic preoccupation with its own image and contemplate instead the physical, emotional, and mental conditions from which the play of self emerges is, for Buddha, "the direct path . . . for the attainment of the true way, for the realization of nirvana."

To experience in depth the natural unfolding of life, Buddha suggests returning to the heart of nature herself: "to the forest, to the root of a tree or to an empty hut." Bearing no trace of human presence or dominion, the anarchy of wilderness is a selfless realm. Trees, shrubs, and creepers sprout, flourish, and wither unimpeded by human design. The poignancy of an empty hut—already perhaps half smothered with foliage—is a stark reminder that no one is there. In contrast to a world saturated with marks of ownership and ambition, nature effortlessly and unintentionally discloses the exfoliation of the same life that pulses through our veins and fills our lungs.

To dwell in the solitude of nature or withdraw to an empty room is not in itself sufficient to still the mad rush of thoughts and emotions that prevent one from settling in contemplation. As Pascal and Montaigne discovered, such solitude tends only to amplify the mind's restlessness. Mara cannot be overcome simply by removing oneself from situations one finds disturbing. Initially it might seem as if retreating from the world makes one *more* distracted. The "runaway horse" of the mind needs to be harnessed to an activity to which one can constantly return. For Montaigne, this was the discipline of writing essays; for Buddha, it was the practice of attending to the inflow and outflow of the breath.

Breathing meditation renders you intimately aware of a primal rhythm of your physical existence. Rather than imaginatively dissecting the body to examine it from without, one feels one's way inside to explore it from within. Having found a stable posture in which the back is upright, bring the totality of attention to the physical sensation of the breath as it enters the nostrils, fills the lungs, pauses, contracts the lungs, is exhaled, pauses, and so on. Do not control the breath; just rest with calm curiosity in an awareness of the body breathing. If the breath is short and shallow, then notice it to be short and shallow. If it is long and deep, notice it to be long and deep. There is no right or wrong way to breathe.

Breathing is a self-regulating motor function of the body. For the most part we draw and exhale breath as effortlessly as a plant turns toward the light of the sun. This natural process happens of its own accord. But as soon as one pays attention to it, its free flow tends to be inhibited by the grip of self-consciousness. Even though you try not to control the breath, the very act of paying attention to it seems to impose a degree of control. The trick is to learn how to remain fully aware of the breath without that awareness impeding its natural ebb and flow.

One way to do this is to *wait* for the breath to happen. After each inhalation and exhalation, there follows a brief pause as the muscles change gear, as it were, before releasing the pent-up air or drawing a fresh breath. The self-consciousness of breathing is most pronounced at these two moments: suddenly it feels as though "I" must exhale or inhale. To dispel this sense of agency, during each pause remain a disinterested observer, curious to notice when and how the muscles will engage of their own accord to initiate the next inbreath or outbreath. Just wait for the next phase in the breathing to kick in: with no expectation as to when it should start, no preparation for it to be deep or shallow, no anticipation for it to be forceful or gentle.

In this open space of alert but disinterested waiting, the organism will suddenly be felt to exhale or inhale on its own. With practice, one learns how to refine one's role as a participating but noninterfering observer of one's breath. In paying careful and sustained attention to the rhythmic sensations of breathing, not only does the mind become more still and focused but one becomes aware of the subtlety and complexity of the process. Any notion of the breath as a quasi-mechanical bellows action of the lungs is replaced by a keen sense of the breath as the body's tidal rhythm, its vital link with the world beyond its skin.

This steady, reassuring rhythm of the breath is the anchor to which one returns each time the mind is snatched away by daydreams or memories. Its fluctuations—from long, serene draughts to brief, jagged gasps—serve as a barometer of one's mood. The breath opens the door to a heightened awareness of the body's inner life: the pulsing, trembling, rushing, itching, tingling, straining, hurting. In probing this medley of sensations, we recognize it as the fabric of which emotion and feeling are woven. A pang of anxiety or a rush of exhilaration appears as a contraction or eruption at a precise location in the body. More diffuse moods such as sadness or contentment seem to be spread like a mist through the entire system, while a gnawing sensation in the solar plexus provokes a familiar but unnameable disquiet. Even the most fugitive thoughts seem to race and sparkle within the bounds of the flesh.

Once settled in the perspective of a still, open awareness, then slowly widen the field of awareness to encompass the texture of clothing against our skin; the polyphony of sounds within and around us; the shifting patches of light, shade, and color; the lingering tastes on our palate; the smells that waft our way. Just as the flame of a candle illuminates a room more vividly when its restless flickering is stilled, so does the mind illuminate experience more clearly when it settles into a calm and equanimous repose. The stillness of mindfulness is not one of trancelike absorption, where attention remains locked on a single object, but an expansive restfulness in which a radiant and supple clarity attends to whatever appears.

And whatever appears, disappears. The closer one attends to the unfolding of life, from thoughts that flit through one's brain to the serene blue canopy of a cloudless sky, the more the inconstancy of things becomes apparent. Everything that presents itself to us through the senses is in motion. A thought races by with such speed that we barely catch it, and the sky changes color with such stately slowness that it seems immobile, but both are equally in flux. Whether it be due to the organism's preference for perceptual constancy or our anxious craving for stability in an uncertain world, we consistently fail to notice this. It is as though our resistance to impermanence is a reflex of that deeper resistance to death. Not only is Mara the resistance, he is the impermanence and death as well.

An eternally vanishing world will never stay fixed in place long enough to satisfy the desires of a self or society for permanent stability and well-being. Yet we instinctively look to such a world as though it were capable of providing such happiness. This deep-seated utopian longing would appear to have biological as well as psychological origins. The evolutionary success of human beings is in part due to our conceptual capacity to anticipate and plan for a future in which we, our kin, and offspring will thrive and prosper.

The success of this strategy requires the notion of an enduring self that is not destroyed by the flux and turbulence of life. Only in this way can "I" and "we" still be around to enjoy the fruits of our efforts when the future arrives. But as we carefully examine the unfolding patterns of life within and around us, no such self can be found. Although this nugget of "me" might feel at times more solid and real than anything else, it evaporates like a mirage as soon as we seek to pin it down. Contrary to expectation, the self lurks neither among the swirling play of events nor apart from them in a realm of its own. As one settles into a contemplative acceptance of the selfless flux of experience, one discovers that, just like the breath, it too happens of its own accord. Even the observing awareness is a momentary consequence of sense data impacting the organs of a complex nervous system capable of representing those data as "things-observed-by-me."

After years of struggle, Buddha discovered how a still and penetrating observation of the transient, painful, unreliable, and selfless nature of experience can release that anxious grip on self and world that lies at the root of existential anguish. The release of the grip (even for a few moments) is nirvana—while the grip, of course, is Mara. In the same way as Buddha needs to conquer Mara in order to be Buddha, so nirvana needs the stilling of samsara in order to be nirvana. And just as Mara haunts Buddha, so samsara haunts nirvana.

15

Learning to Wait

IF THE DEVIL'S CIRCLE spins consoling fictions of a
self and world that are unambiguous, controllable, and self-
evident, then nirvana, as the stilling of that spin, discloses a
self and world that are ambiguous, uncontrollable, and perplexing. The release of nirvana rests in a serene astonishment
at a fleeting self and world that simultaneously reveal themselves and withdraw. "Do you know who it is," asks Lin-chi,

> who right now is running around searching this way? He
> is brisk and lively, with no roots at all. Though you em-
> brace him, you cannot gather him in; though you drive
> him away, you cannot shake him off. If you seek him, he
> retreats farther and farther away; if you don't seek him,
> then he's right there before your eyes.

No matter how deeply one probes life, no matter how much one knows about it, will it not still remain a question for you? Will not something about it forever elude your grasp? Could not the most precise scientific equations, the sublimest music, poetry, and art, the profoundest teachings of the world's religions and philosophies be but tufts of cotton thrown into the wind of the question: "Why is there anything at all?"

When the monk Radha asked, "What is the purpose of nirvana?" Buddha replied:

> You have gone beyond the range of questioning, Radha. You weren't able to grasp the limit to questioning. For the divine life, Radha, is lived with nirvana as its ground, nirvana as its destination, nirvana as its final goal.

As a crack in the edifice of samsara, a momentary loosening of Mara's grip, or the unimpeded ease of each breath, nirvana comes unbidden. We are shocked out of habitual certainties into a sense of the world as uncanny and unreliable. This perplexity is the first hazy intimation of nirvana. Its intensity does not agitate us but is cradled in a strange stillness. Whether it crystallizes into a question like "What is this thing?" or coagulates into a gnawing sensation of doubt in the belly, it becomes the source and ground of a path.

In contrast to the anguished restlessness of samsara, the release of nirvana is experienced as ease. Such ease is a feature not merely of Buddha's inner life but of the effortless unfolding of life itself. "Whatever is contingent," says Nagarjuna, "is naturally at ease." This nirvanic ease is already present in the selfless, unimpeded play of the natural world: the unfurling of a leaf, the spring of a cat, the trickle of a stream. To symbolize his conquest of Mara, Buddha touches the earth. Nirvana is not located in a remote celestial realm; it is rooted in the ground of our own being. However solid, opaque, and resistant this ground might at first seem, as we calmly attend to it, it opens up as a groundlessness of infinite depth and ease. As a result, says Shantideva, "living beings are naturally nirvanic."

Perplexity is an appropriate response to this ground whose groundlessness is like an abyss from which all things spring forth. But to call this ground the "Sublime" or "One Mind," "Emptiness," or "God" is to risk being ensnared once more by Mara. For rather than resting in the boundless unknown that animates perplexity, we return to the safe bounds of a concept that we believe we understand. Instead of embracing the ineffability of our existence, we scramble for the consolation of a manageable religious or philosophical idea. One must be prepared to relinquish even the minimal consolation of a "groundless ground."

You just wait in the abyss of perplexity without expecting anything. You open yourself to the uncanniness of what unfolds without construing it as this or that. You abandon any notion of a result of such practice. In exhorting his followers to "kill Buddha," Lin-chi insists that we rid the mind of every image or idea we have ever had of awakening. "If you seek Buddha," he declares, "you'll be held in the grip of the Buddha-Mara." However noble, refined, and erudite one's idea of Buddha, it can never be more than a collage of memories and concepts drawn from your own and others' past experience. It encloses you in the realm of what is already known.

Instead of settling into a calm awareness of the effortless unfolding of experience, part of us strives to be already one step ahead of ourselves. Mara is impatient. He is never content to sit still and wait. His goal is always to be elsewhere. Like a print which is slightly out of register, our wraithlike double strains to slip off into an alternative world. The unease of such restlessness lies in this rebellious longing to be elsewhere when it is impossible to be anywhere but here. In making a concerted effort to remain *here* by returning again and again to the present moment, it is as though we are deliberately provoking the devil.

The forces that Mara summons to strike back are sensual desire, ill-will, restlessness, torpor, and doubt. These hindrances "lead away from nirvana" by destroying the calm, focused awareness of what is unfolding here and now. One moment we are mindfully attending to the breath or asking "What is this thing?" only in the next to be besieged by an erotic fantasy or a furious resentment. Or our equanimity is rattled by a visceral anxiety; or we slump into a mire of lethargy; or niggling doubts resurface to mock our convictions and aims. Once possessed by these demons, the mind quickly loses its natural suppleness and radiancy and becomes brittle, dull, and unfocused. Buddha describes such hindrances as "encirclers of the mind," comparing them to giant creepers that bind themselves round other trees, making their hosts "bent, twisted and split." Once more we find ourselves enclosed in Mara's snare.

Just as a waiter attends to the needs of those at the table he serves, so one waits with unknowing astonishment at the quixotic play of life. In subordinating his own wants to those of the customer, a waiter abandons any expectation of what he may be next called to do. Constantly alert and ready to respond, the oddest request does not faze him. He neither ignores those he serves nor appears at the wrong time. He is invisible but always there when needed. Likewise, in asking "What is this thing?" one does not strain ahead of oneself in anticipation of a result. One waits at ease for a response one cannot foresee and that might never come. The most one can "do" is remain optimally receptive and alert.

We hate waiting. When a train doesn't come on time or if a friend is late, we find ourselves frustrated by a situation over which we have no control. Rather than things happening according to plan, we are suddenly at the mercy of someone else and powerless to influence the outcome of events. As the consoling illusion of a dependable and manageable world evaporates with each passing second, we are exposed to the anguish of life's intrinsic unreliability. Our impatience mounts, the self's composure crumbles into resentful frustration or erupts into panic, and we are exposed as an infantile creature of Mara.

Instead of regarding it either as an affront to one's dignity or a waste of time, waiting can be seen as a cipher of nirvana. Since life is ultimately a situation over which we have no control, waiting is a response that accords with its fleeting and unreliable nature. The practice of waiting is to learn how to rest in the nirvanic ease of contingent things. Yet waiting is not passive inaction any more than emptiness is nothingness. As an alert stillness that cradles perplexity, it is the ground from which we can respond in unpredictable ways to life's unfolding and the inevitable encounter with others.

THREE

LIVING WITH THE DEVIL

16

An Ordinary Person's Life

TO LIVE WITH THE DEVIL is to plunge into this elusive, beguiling, obstructive, giddying, unreliable, bewitching, sublimely ephemeral world. To survive in the midst of such dazzling contingency requires that one understand, tolerate, and love this world. For were the world not this way, there would be no path, no awakening, no nirvana, no freedom. Mara and Buddha are entwined with each other. To pretend that either can exist in isolation is to fall prey to Mara's oldest trick: tearing a conditioned thing out of the matrix in which it lives and raising it to the status of an unconditioned truth.

If Mara is death, then, as his polar opposite, Buddha is life. The Evil One and the Awakened One are as inseparable from each other as death is from life. Life without death and death without life are meaningless. Life is what it is because it streams irrevocably and magnificently toward its end. The pouring forth of each living thing in its fecund, glorious excess is also its death throe. To live is to surrender to one's end. One gives oneself over to responding to the question of being here at all—in the knowledge that each day, each hour, each minute may be your last chance to do this. Like the blowing out of a flame, nirvana is life's extinguishing of itself each moment.

Without the devil to obstruct it, one could not create a path. For a path is kept open by overcoming the hindrances that prevent freedom of movement along it. If Mara did not get in the way, there would be nothing to give us the purchase we need to propel ourselves out of a crisis. Were there no circular drift to our lives, there would be no need for a guiding vision to orient ourselves; if we were not frustrated, there would be no need to break out of a rut; were there no isolation, then no need to participate in communities of shared ideas and practices; and without conflict or contradiction, no possibility of achieving harmony or resolution.

Rather than gaining insight into a single Absolute Truth, Buddha awoke to a complex of truths that embraced the conflicts of human existence as well as their resolution. This awakening did not leave him stranded in a permanent mystical enlightenment, but opened up for him a path to follow in the midst of the world's vicissitudes. The impact Buddha had on those who encountered him was not solely due to his wise words and compassionate acts. For it seems that he appeared to others as someone in whom something had stopped in a radical and startling manner.

When the serial killer Angulimala tried to add Buddha to his string of victims, he waylaid him on the road and chased after him. But no matter how fast he ran, he could not catch up with the calmly walking monk. So he shouted, "Stop! Stop!" Buddha said, "I have stopped. Now you stop," explaining, "I have stopped forever. I abstain from violence toward beings; but you have no restraint toward things that live: that is why I have stopped and you have not." So impressed was the killer that he threw away his weapons and asked to become a monk.

Each interaction between Buddha and Mara (or his proxy such as Angulimala) dramatizes abstract ideas by turning them into the interplay between human characters. The tensions between samsara and nirvana, fixation and freedom, start to crackle with immediacy. What is at stake bursts into life. It is this vitality that makes stories more compelling than theories. One's own life is mirrored in these dramas in a way that no amount of theorizing can achieve.

Te-shan was a ninth century Chinese scholar monk renowned for his knowledge of the monastic rule and as an authority on Buddha's *Diamond Sutra*. One day he was incensed to learn that a new school called Ch'an (Zen) was flourishing in the south of the country. "How dare these southern devils say that just by pointing at the human mind one can see one's nature and become a buddha?" he remonstrated. "I'll go drag them from their caves and exterminate their ilk, and thus repay the kindness of Buddha." With his books on his back, he set off on his mission.

On reaching the town of Li-chou, Te-shan put down his bundle of texts and approached an old woman who was selling refreshments by the roadside. Eyeing his stack of books, she said,

> I will only serve you if you can answer my question. The *Diamond Sutra* says "past mind can't be grasped, present mind can't be grasped, future mind can't be grasped." Which mind does the learned monk desire to refresh?

Te-shan was speechless. Aware of the inadequacy of his knowledge, he followed the old woman's advice to seek out Lung-t'an, one of the Zen teachers he had come to persecute. One dark night as he was about to leave the master's quarters, Lung-t'an offered him a candle to light his way. As Te-shan reached for it, Lung-t'an blew it out. Te-shan was suddenly awakened to what Buddha had taught. The following day he set fire to his texts and spent the next thirty years in obscurity practicing meditation.

Buddha and Christ may have conquered the devil, but that does not prevent the devil from corrupting Buddhism or Christianity. The theme of the *Diamond Sutra* is a liberating vision of emptiness. Te-shan turned it into a doctrine of oppression. He could not tolerate the suggestion that Buddha might infuse ordinary life. For him, Buddha and emptiness had become isolated from the turbulent, contingent flux of existence and placed out of reach on the pedestal of Truth. Mara had succeeded in making his own what was intended to defeat him. As the "imposer of limits" (*Antaka*), he enclosed emptiness within the confines of a religious doctrine that its believers would fight to uphold.

Zen sought to reconquer Mara by rejecting these divisions and affirming Buddha at the heart of the everyday. In the sensuous, painful flux of the here and now, Buddha is neither silent nor alone but in endless conversation with the devil. Mara is not rejected or condemned but embraced and transformed. Buddha accepts his incarnation in the diabolic stuff of existence. He knows that every moment "Mara's stream" is slipping away and in the end will destroy him. But he neither gets entangled in it nor recoils from it. Thus are fears and desires, frustrations and doubts transformed from hindrances into catalysts of understanding and freedom.

By the time he emerged from his retreat, Te-shan had abandoned his idealistic view of Buddha. "What is awakening?" asked a monk. "Get out!" said Te-shan. "Don't defecate here." "And Buddha?" persisted the monk. "An old Indian beggar," said Te-shan. Once he told his assembly:

> Here, there are no ancestors and no buddhas. Bodhidharma is a stinking foreigner. Shakyamuni is a dried-up piece of shit. "Awakening" and "nirvana" are posts to tether donkeys. The scriptural canon was written by

devils; it's just paper for wiping infected skin boils. None of these things will save you.

He sought to dispel any lingering attachment to Buddha as something to be found apart from the messiness of the everyday. He had no time for the grandiose conceits of religion. "What is known as 'realizing the mystery,'" he said, "is nothing but breaking through to grab an ordinary person's life."

Like other Zen teachers of his time, Te-shan sought to shock his audience into seeing that Buddha was not a remote historical figure to be venerated as a saint, but a vital presence in the pulsing heart of each living creature. Declared Lin-chi,

In this lump of raw flesh is a true person of no status continually going in and out of the face of each one of you. Those who have not confirmed this, Look! Look!

Lin-chi sought to awaken the innate responsiveness of his students that shines forth just before the anesthetic of self-consciousness takes hold. When a monk in the gathering asked him to explain what he meant, Lin-chi came down from his seat, grabbed the man, and yelled, "Speak! Speak!" The monk hesitated and Lin-chi shoved him aside, muttering, "The true person of no status—what a caked shit-stick."

The "true person of no status" evokes the ambiguity of each human being we encounter. "True person" (chen-jen) was the common Chinese term for an awakened sage, whereas to have "no status" in the China of Lin-chi's time was to be marginalized as a nobody. In the face of another person, we simultaneously glimpse a natural dignity as well as the anguish of one who is radically unsure of his place in the scheme of things. To recognize Buddha in the eyes of each person we meet is to engage with another who silently calls upon us to respond to her buddhanature.

17

"Do Not Hurt Me"

PEOPLE STREAM TOWARD YOU on the sidewalk of a city street. With each approaching step, a human singularity gathers into sharper relief until for a tantalizing moment she stands exposed before you: red lips sealed tight in a sea of wrinkled skin, the sharp aquiline nose, a darkly shining inwardness of eyes, strands of disobedient hair across a furrowed brow. The face reveals a contradictory person: loved, admired, disliked, and feared by others as you are, who could have been but never will be known. In a blur she is gone.

Just as you peer out beyond yourself to scrutinize others, so do they gaze from their interiority to wonder about you. The curiosity and rapid sideways glance when our eyes accidentally meet are mutual. Consciousness is keenly impacted by the uncontrollable presence of others. Otherness reaches its apotheosis in the face of that most familiar and strange of beings:

someone else. A stranger has the power to discharge inside one a rush of loathing or longing that can make one sweat and tremble. The lineaments of a face can suggest a lifetime of intimacies to be given or withheld, accepted or rejected.

Like myself, each sentient creature I encounter is in pursuit of a path. The glint in their eyes reflects an anguished concern with goals and obstacles. Even a fly, restlessly probing the pane of glass that stands in its way, speaks to my condition. Others are the mirror in which I most vividly glimpse myself. The consciousness of being the person we are unfolds from our interactions with others. One's identity is not given ready-made at birth. It emerges when a configuration of inborn potentiality is subjected to the identities and desires of others: parents, siblings, educators, priests, rulers, enemies, role models. I understand myself in concepts and phrases that belong not to me but to the linguistic community of which I am a member. The internal monologue of a self is intended as much for others as for myself.

Incessant social intercourse continues unabated even when we are alone with our thoughts far from other people. We compulsively nuance the definition of ourselves through shared words, images, and codes. The concept of self is intelligible only in relation to the concept of other. However vividly I seem to stand apart from you, without you there would be nothing from which I could stand apart. "I" without "you" makes as little sense as "here" without "there." Asserting a separate self affirms participation in a world of others even as one tries to deny it.

In the naked glimpse of another's face, we encounter both a fear of and yearning for intimacy. A core paradox of human existence is that we are inescapably alone and at the same time inescapably a participant in a world with others. While we long for intimacy in order to dispel loneliness, we resist it because it threatens to interrupt our privacy. Just as Mara prompts us to flee the overwhelming contingency of our birth and death to the safety of an isolated self, so he urges us to flee the disruptive impact that intimacy might have upon such a self. And just as Buddha's wisdom springs from focusing attention unwaveringly upon the turbulent flux of contingency, so his compassion springs from returning the intimate gaze of the other that implores you not to hurt her.

If flight is a retreat from intimacy, then fixation on one's self and one's obsessions is a way of denying it. Rather than opening to another, you close down behind a frozen gaze and expression so as not to betray insecurity or fear. Even as she speaks to you, concern with how you appear outweighs your attention to what she says. The poses and disguises we assume to make an impression on others conceal our ambivalence as to who we are. Rather than confront the unfathomable question of our existence, we seal ourselves in the membrane of a story that we know only sketches our surface. As long as we can convince ourselves and others of the reliability and value of this narrative, we feel safe.

To behold another's face is to tolerate a gaze even as I glance aside in shame. Whereas to smile compliantly while studying the complexion of the face's skin, judging the attractiveness of its features, or trying to decipher what conclusions about us are being drawn behind its façade is no longer to encounter one another. In Martin Buber's terms, the "you" has been replaced by an "it." But when we relate to another as "you,"

> he is not a point in the world net of space and time, nor
> a construct that can be experienced and described. . . .
> Neighborless and seamless, he is you and fills the circle
> of the sky.

Just as Mara's strategies reduce the other to a manageable "it," thereby avoiding the threat of intimacy, Buddha's perspective opens up the limitless vista of an ineffable "you," thus making it possible to encounter the other without hesitation.

Even when no words are spoken, your face calls out to me. "The first word of the face," says the Jewish philosopher Emmanuel Levinas, "is the 'Thou shalt not kill.'"

> It is an order. There is a commandment in the appear-
> ance of the face, as if a master spoke to me. At the same
> time, the face of the Other is destitute; it is the poor for
> whom I can do all and to whom I owe all.

We recognize this call because we hear in it the echo of our own deepest fears and longings. Another's face shocks us into a helpless silence in which we are called to respond from the same depth within ourselves that we witness in his plea. In the very instant that we hear Mara prompting us to utter a consoling cliché, a religious platitude, or a gem of psychotherapeutic wisdom, we hear Buddha urging us to let go of the self-consciousness that paralyzes a selfless response.

The roots of empathy, compassion, and love lie in that intimate encounter where we hear the other wordlessly say

> do not kill me, do not rob me, do not abuse me, do not
> deceive me, do not betray me, do not insult me, do not
> waste my time, do not try to possess me, do not bear me
> ill will, do not misconstrue me.

These pleas are the foundation of an ethics that Buddhism describes as "natural" as opposed to "entailed." Prior to the adoption of beliefs or commitments that entail moral obligations, the other naturally calls upon you not to harm her. While a vow might entail a commitment to celibacy or monogamy, such specific injunctions are not present in the call of the other. Others simply enjoin us not to hurt them. Only in responding to their command do additional religious, social, and legal conventions come into play.

On hearing the silent "do not hurt me," we are called to risk responding to that plea. Even when someone threatens us in a voice shaking with rage, his mute cry can still be heard beneath the torrent of abuse. In spite of itself, violent emotion can render the plea more audible than when it is stifled behind a carefully honed façade of contentment. Instead of fueling a spiral of mutual hatred by returning the insult, we are free to respond to the other's deeper injunction not to hurt him. In moments of intimacy, we find ourselves no longer in the grip of self-consciousness but in a free and open space whence we respond to the other in ways that astonish us. When such constraints are suspended, we recover an ease that allows us to spontaneously engage with the other's dilemma.

To suffer with someone else, to imagine what it feels like for him inside the envelope of his skin, is not only a sign of our shared sentience. I find myself open to an otherness that is forever beyond my reach and control. I cannot know him in the way he knows himself, any more than he can know me in the way I know myself. The moment when mutual recognition dawns includes an awareness of what is unknowable: what it is like for him to see me with his eyes, hear me with his ears, think of me in his brain.

In encountering another, one is confronted not with an immutable fact but a pathway of possible intimacy. One speaks of someone being "closed" or "open," of "getting through" to them, of finding the "chinks in his armor." A person is like a path: a space whose trajectory we may or may not be invited to share. We long to trust others enough to dismantle the boundaries we initially want them to respect. To be intimate with another is to be allowed inside their life and to let them enter yours. As we embark on the seemingly endless quest of mutual understanding, we become a chapter in each other's story, figures in each other's dreams, creators of each other's self. To know another intimately is not achieved by dissolving the differences between us but by allowing the space to draw them out. Such differentiation is realized through probing and being probed by the otherness of the other.

In letting someone else into your life, you open yourself to the risk of being astonished. For intimacy to remain alive, the other must remain a mystery for you. To know someone intimately is to honor them as embodying an unknown. However well you know and trust them, you cannot afford the complacency of taking them for granted. A beloved partner in a life-long relationship can be capricious and unpredictable. When caught in Mara's snare you prefer not to see this. Over time, you tend to enclose the other within limits that define them according to your own needs and desires.

18

The Anguish of Others

"A MONK WAS SICK with dysentery," records a passage in the Pali Canon, "and lay fouled in his own urine and excrement." Buddha came to his lodging and asked why no one was taking care of him. "The other monks don't care for me," he replied, "because I do nothing for them." Buddha and his attendant Ananda washed the monk, lifted him up, and laid him on a bed. Having questioned the community about its failure to care for the sick monk, Buddha said, "Monks, you have no mother or father who might tend to you. If you do not tend to one another, then who will tend to you? Whoever would tend to me, should tend to the sick."

Through intimately identifying himself with the sick monk, Buddha affirms the link between the questions that prompted his quest and the awakening in which it culminated. Without birth, sickness, ageing, and death, there would be neither awakening (*bodhi*) nor an awakened one (*buddha*). Awakening is only intelligible as a response to the diabolic contingency of the human condition. Buddha can identify with the sick monk because he can see his own awakening prefigured in the other's suffering. He shows his monks the contradiction in honoring him while ignoring their sick brother. Awakening, he implies, is rooted in the anguish of a man lying uncared for on the ground in a pool of his own piss and shit.

When Jesus describes the final reckoning on the day of the Last Judgment, he identifies himself with every suffering person. In summoning the righteous to eternal life, he depicts himself as saying to them:

> For I was hungry, and ye gave me meat: I was thirsty, and
> ye gave me drink: I was a stranger, and ye took me in:
> Naked, and ye clothed me: I was sick, and ye visited me:
> I was in prison, and ye came unto me.

His listeners are baffled; they have no recollection of treating him in this way. "Inasmuch as ye have done it unto one of the least of these my brethren," explains Jesus, "ye have done it unto me." Both Buddha and Christ insist that the path they advocate leads not away from the singular anguish of others but into its heart.

Mara's obsession with limits is driven in part by the intuitive terror of having to face the limitless suffering of others. In conquering Mara, Buddha's awakening exposed him to the raw, unfiltered anguish of the other. In freeing himself from compulsive, self-centered reactivity, he exposed himself to the unpredictable demands of his world. His achievement was not merely one of dwelling in this unbounded emptiness but having the capacity to *tolerate* it. Such tolerance occurs, explains Robert Thurman, when "the mind reaches a stage where it can bear its lack of bearings, . . . can endure this kind of extreme openness."

In freeing oneself from the limiting and ensnaring effects of "me" and "mine," such emptiness confronts one with the turbulent and intimidating needs of others against which one seeks to immunize oneself with the reassuring conviction of being a static, isolated self. In meeting another's gaze, you come to recognize a trembling concentration of contingencies as inconceivably complex and singular as your own. The experience of emptiness affords more than insight into the nature of contingency; it opens the way to an empathetic connection with others beyond the narrow orbit of family, friends, and lovers.

To illustrate how a selfless, contingent reality is also one of empathetic interconnectivity, Shantideva imagines the whole of life to be like a single body in which each creature is a distinct but integral part. He aspires to respond to the plight of others with the same sympathetic empathy that connects different parts of the body. "Why does the hand protect the foot," he asks, "when the pain of the foot is not that of the hand?" As though in reply, Meister Eckhart says, "If the foot could speak, it would say that the eye, though located in the head, is as much its own as if it were located in the foot, and the eye in turn would say the same thing." Each part instinctively identifies with other parts of the same whole. "When someone steps on another's foot," says Eckhart, "it is the tongue that says, 'You stepped on me.'"

So why when I see a stranger in evident distress do I hesitate to reach out and comfort him? Why do I avoid looking him in the eye? This reluctance is an acutely disquieting compound of sympathy, guilt, and shyness accompanied by a flustered litany of good reasons for not getting involved. In the moment of turning away from the other, I feel the sting of intimacy betrayed. For Buddhists, this discomfort may be compounded by the failure to have tended to the other as Buddha. As a Christian, one may be aware of failing to have treated the other as Christ.

We enclose ourselves in a circle of self-interest, like a hand unaware of the rest of the body to which it belongs. "This separated member," explains Pascal,

> believes itself to be a whole and, seeing no body on which it depends, believes itself to be dependent only on itself and tries to make itself its own center and body. But, not having in itself any principle of life, it only wanders about and is shocked by the uncertainty of its existence.

The plight of both Mara and Satan is to be banished from life itself. My sense of alienation is likewise rooted in this numbness to interconnectivity. I feel as though I haunt the world rather than participate in it. Even as I chatter in the midst of company, I feel eerily disengaged.

Then in the next moment I find myself startled by the suffering of another as though it were my own. In this glimpse of intimacy, we experience the astonishment of belonging again to a body of life that infinitely exceeds our own. The numbness of alienation gives way to the astonishment of participation. The closure of Mara is replaced by the openness of Buddha. Intimacy is realized in wholly giving oneself while wholly receiving the gift of the other.

The experience of sympathetic empathy dissolves not only one's sense of isolation but any need to justify one's feelings and actions in terms of an ideology. One does not care for the sick because Buddha said that "whoever would tend to me, should tend to the sick" or because it will propel one along the path toward awakening. One takes care of them because they are ill. For Shantideva, such behavior "is just like feeding oneself; one hopes for nothing in return."

Jesus places his followers in a similar double bind. He describes the righteous who will attain eternal life as those who feed the hungry and clothe the naked *without being aware* that they are feeding or clothing Christ. One feeds the hungry and clothes the naked simply because they are hungry and naked, not because by doing so one will be rewarded with eternal life. Religious belief may encourage one to become more compassionate, but it can compromise the heartfelt spontaneity of compassion. To realize Buddhist compassion or Christian love may entail suspending one's identity as a Buddhist or a Christian.

No matter how carefully we attend to the call of the other, it is incapable of telling us *how* to respond. While unequivocably called upon to act, we are uncertain what to do. It is not just a question of obeying the explicit command that reaches our ears—the plea of an alcoholic to buy him a drink contradicts the mute plea not to harm him. So we meditate in the hope of hearing the wisdom of a quiet inner voice or pray for divine guidance, only to be greeted by silence. Even if we "hear" something, how do we know it is not the prompting of the devil? If we trust it, we still must decide whether, when, and how to act on it. In the end we, rather than our buddha-nature or god, will be held responsible for what we do. The dilemma of choice is inescapable.

Whether it be the Jewish Talmud or Buddhist Vinaya, no system of rules and prohibitions, however elaborate, can provide exact instructions on how to deal with an unprecedented moral dilemma. We may be enjoined not to kill, but when the life of a mother is at risk, is it acceptable to terminate the life of her unborn child in order to save hers? Or do we let nature follow its course and allow the woman to die? Whose silent "do not hurt me" takes precedence? The mother's? Or the child's? At best, ethical precepts provide a coherent framework for guiding one's actions; at worst, they encourage a self-righteous legalism that pays no heed to the call of the other.

To act is to risk. The contingency and complexity of life is such that we cannot foresee what will happen next. What seems a misfortune today (being crippled) turns out to be a blessing tomorrow (when all able-bodied men are rounded up and killed). We act with the noblest intentions, having carefully weighed our options, only to make matters worse. Finding your kind smile and wise words patronizing and hollow, your friend perversely chooses to do the opposite of what you suggest.

19

Incarnation

MILAN KUNDERA'S NOVEL *Immortality* opens with the narrator (who may or may not be the author—we later discover that he is a writer who has published a book with the same title as one of Kundera's) sitting in a deck chair by the pool at his health club, observing an old woman having a swimming lesson. When the lesson is over, she walks toward the exit, then turns her head, smiles, and waves goodbye to her young instructor. "At that instant," recalls the narrator, "I felt a pang in my heart. That smile and that gesture belonged to a twenty-year-old girl! Her hand reached out with a ravishing lightness." The smile and wave had "the charm of a gesture drowning in the charmlessness of the body." Then this charm crystallizes into the name "Agnes," and the central character of the novel, whose life and sudden death are described in intimate detail over the next four hundred pages, is incarnated in the narrator's mind.

Agnes was born from the imagination of a storyteller. Each new piece of information we acquire about her is like a brush-stroke that highlights another feature of her character. We swiftly and effortlessly build up a portrait of Agnes until we feel that we know what it would be like to be her. On learning that she has died in a car crash, we feel shocked and saddened.

Intuitively, we think of Agnes as a disembodied essence incarnated ("enfleshed") in a body. The more we learn about her, the closer we come to penetrating the mysterious heart of who she is. She comes into focus through a steady accumulation of detail that configures an increasingly unique blend of different traits. This configuration is not the medium through which Agnes makes herself known. For there is no Agnes apart from the configuration of these traits. Agnes is the incarnation of the contingencies of her life: the accidents of her birth, the chances she takes, the choices she makes, the things that happen to her.

The only difference between Agnes and a nonfictional person like yourself is that you incarnate contingencies that can be traced to a body and its impact on others. Agnes has no fingerprints that could link her to the scene of a crime. Agnes has no dental record or DNA profile that could identify her remains in a burnt-out car. Were her character further fleshed out, she could be movingly portrayed in a play or film. But

Agnes cannot be photographed. For a photograph presents material evidence that something took place in the world we share. The unrepeatable way in which light reflected off that face or building or landscape fifty years ago is still fixed in the emulsion of the negative. A photograph, writes Susan Sontag, "is a material vestige of its subject in a way that no painting can be." Even a poorly exposed and blurred snapshot is "a trace, something directly stenciled off the real, like a footprint or a deathmask." A photograph is a "drawing" (*graphos*) in "light" (*phos* > *photo-*).

"All novels," writes Kundera, "are concerned with the enigma of self." Each character is an opportunity for the novelist to undertake a "meditative interrogation" of this self. Yet "the more powerful the lens of the microscope observing the self, the more the self and its uniqueness elude us." This elusive self possesses an unbearable lightness, both playful and tragic at once, that can slip away or be destroyed at any moment. Tereza, another Kunderan character, looks into a mirror and wonders how long it would take for her to vanish if her nose were to grow by a millimeter a day. "If her face no longer looked like Tereza," the author asks, "would Tereza still be Tereza? Where does the self begin and end?" Kundera's sense of wonder is not about "the immeasurable infinity of the soul" but "the uncertain nature of the self and its identity."

Our incarnation in this world unfolds from an eerie collision between unprecedented physical contingencies and those stories we endlessly tell about ourselves and others. We identify and empathize with Agnes and Tereza because we share their storylike nature. People get to know us through our stories much in the same way they come to empathize with a character in a play or novel. As anyone can attest who has been emotionally transported by a film, profound moments of intimacy can occur in the company of fictional beings. At the same time, we are irreducibly different from them because, like Milan Kundera, we pose and grin and have photographs to prove it.

Buddha (who is neither quite the same as nor entirely different from Gotama) became incarnate only when he began to tell the story of his awakening to others. His initial impulse was not even to try communicating what he had discovered. "This dharma I have attained," he reflected,

> is profound, hard to see and understand, peaceful and sublime, unattainable by mere reasoning, subtle, to be experienced by the wise. . . . If I were to teach the dharma, others would not understand me, and that would be wearying and troublesome for me.

But the god Brahma (the creator of the world in traditional Indian cosmology) was reading his mind and immediately vanished from the heavens and appeared before Buddha to persuade him to teach those "with little dust in their eyes who are wasting through not hearing the dharma." And so "out of compassion for beings," Buddha began to translate the ineffable depths of contingency and emptiness into the slippery ambiguities of language and forms of life.

Unless we are prepared to regard Brahma as a celestial apparition who descends from the sky in order to plead with Buddha on behalf of humanity, we need to consider him as another metaphor of Buddha's inner life. If Mara represents Buddha's shadow, then Brahma represents his charisma. While Mara appears to Buddha on his deathbed as a reminder of his inescapable mortality, so Brahma appears at the beginning of his career as the inspiration to engage with the world. In both cases Buddha is confronted with his destiny. As an embodied creature he can neither avoid death nor ignore the injunction to heed the call of others who suffer.

Although they frame the parameters of his incarnation, Brahma and Mara are unable to sway Buddha from his nirvanic release. Their appearance as mythic figures interacting with Buddha throughout his life suggests how the divine and demonic are dimensions of the human condition. They are not deleted by awakening but understood for what they are. Buddha acknowledges their presence by granting Brahma and Mara roles in his moral universe, but refuses to take them as seriously as they would like to be taken.

Buddha tells of how he once miraculously vanished from earth and appeared in the realm of Brahma to dissuade the god from believing that the divine condition was eternal. This mythic episode points to Buddha's own struggle with the numinous fascination exerted by the divine. The discourse relates how "Mara took possession of a member of the god's assembly," who said to Buddha:

> Monk, monk, do not disbelieve him; for this Brahma is the Great Brahma, the Overlord, the Untranscended, of Infallible Vision, Wielder of Mastery, Lord Maker and Creator, Most High Providence, Master and Father of those that are and ever can be.

Mara warns that Buddha will fall into a deep chasm should he fail to heed the command of such a being. The devil appears as an echo of Gotama's own doubt that he might suffer divine retribution should he persist in denying the claims of this god. Buddha is unmoved and replies, "I know you, Evil One. You are Mara, and the Brahma and his Assembly . . . have all fallen into your hands, . . . but I have not fallen into your power." In recognizing how the divine and demonic are intertwined, Buddha rejects Brahma's boasts with the same insouciance as he dismisses Mara's threats.

Buddha in his freedom is beyond the reach of either divine or demonic influence, but his incarnation in human history is mediated through gods and devils. Although nirvana may be beyond good and evil, as soon as Buddha stirs from its transcendent ease, he is confronted with the inescapable polarities of moral life. First we find him resting in nirvanic peace; then a "god" intervenes to incite him to compassion; then he decides to head for Benares (Varanasi) to teach his former ascetic companions. Each step takes him further into the ambiguities and vicissitudes of life. His incarnation originates in formlessness, coalesces as polarized images or ideas, then breaks into the sensual world as speech and acts that have repercussions he cannot foresee.

Buddha cannot be adequately understood by describing his state of mind at the moment of awakening any more than Mozart can be understood by describing his state of mind at the moment he is inspired to compose a symphony. To understand either the saint or the artist, that initial, formless moment has to be imaginatively transformed into concrete images or sounds in time and space that are meaningful to others. Mozart first "hears" something in the silence of his own mind, then transcribes it into musical notation so it can be interpreted and played by musicians. Likewise, Buddha undergoes an awakening in silent contemplation beneath a tree, then translates it into ideas so it can be interpreted and practiced by men and women.

The way in which a formless insight achieves abstract and then concrete form is the rhythm of incarnation. Tragically, this rhythm rarely unfolds as freely and luminously as we imagine it did for Buddha and Mozart. When snared by Mara, incarnation is blocked by opaque concepts of self, distorted by compulsive behavior we find hard to resist, shackled by the constraints of a dying body. We rage at our incapacity to express the sublime feelings and intuitions that move us in our wordless depths. The imagery we seek eludes us and we lapse into tired expressions borrowed from others.

The unfolding process of incarnation is captured in Roland Barthes' comment, "who *speaks* is not who *writes,* and who *writes* is not who *is.*" What we *are* is mysterious. The peculiar sense of being here at all, of not being dead, is the most intimate, ineffable, universal, and ecstatic experience we know. At best it can be articulated as an astonished "What?" or "Who?" or "Why?" As thinking creatures, we puzzle over our fate and try to make sense of it. We write poems and essays, compose music, paint pictures, take photos, read books, hold earnest conversations, go to art galleries, play violins, listen to Mozart. The one who does these things is a step removed from the one who sits in meditation waiting for the next in-breath. And the one who shaves each morning and berates the cat is a step removed from the one who writes essays on Buddhist theology.

"It's Borges, the other one," reflects the Argentinian writer Jorge Luis Borges, "that things happen to." Whereas

> I walk through Buenos Aires and I pause—mechanically now perhaps—to gaze at the arch of an entryway and its inner door; news of Borges reaches me by mail, or I see his name on a list of academics or in some biographical dictionary. My taste runs to hourglasses, maps, seventeenth-century typefaces, etymologies, the taste of

coffee, and the prose of Robert Louis Stevenson; Borges shares these preferences, but in a vain sort of way that turns them into accoutrements of an actor.

These parallel beings glide in and out of focus as we pass through the hours and days that make up our lives. Our buddha, gods, and devils rub shoulders with each other. One moment, we are resting in stunned astonishment that there is anything at all; the next, we are composing a line of poetry; and the next, we are tying our shoelaces. Borges concludes his reflection by confessing, "I am not sure which one of us is writing this page."

20

A Culture of Awakening

WHATEVER RUDIMENTS of a system Gotama may have
worked out in his solitude beneath the bodhi tree, how could
he have foreseen the questions and objections that his audience
would put to him? As soon as he faced others and began speaking, he would have been confronted by a torrent of unpredictable contingencies to which he had to respond in ways that
satisfied his listeners' concerns yet stayed true to the inner
compass of his own understanding. Rather than imagining the
dharma as a detailed blueprint preformed in Buddha's mind,
waiting to be implanted in the passive minds of disciples, the
culture of awakening to which he gave birth arose gradually
and haphazardly from the interactions between himself and
his world.

Without this interaction, neither Buddha nor his vision
would have become incarnate. Gotama would have been just

another forgotten Indian sage. One cannot achieve incarnation in a specific time and place without assuming the forms of that time and place. To be intelligible to others, even as one challenges their most cherished beliefs, entails that one speak in terms they understand. Sympathetic empathy required that Buddha operate within the linguistic, cultural, and social paradigms of his time. The price of compassion was to make a pact with the devil: Buddha had to enclose an intuition of what is limitless and signless within conceptual limits and signs, to clothe the "timeless" dharma in the timebound garb of ancient India.

In contrast to popular images of Buddha surrounded by an entourage of monks who hang on his every word, some of the earliest discourses in Pali present him as a solitary figure who wanders from place to place and encourages his followers to be independent of him. Traditionally, a Buddhist monk would spend only five years in the company of his preceptor before going off on his own. "Wander forth, O monks," said Buddha,

> for the welfare of the multitude, for the happiness of the multitude, out of compassion for the world, for the good, welfare, and happiness of gods and humans. *Let no two go the same way.*

Each monk had to make his way through the world on his own, only regrouping with his brethren in shelters during the monsoon period. "The sage who wanders alone," said Buddha, "is like the wind that is not caught in a net, like the lotus not soiled by water, leading others but not led by them."

On another occasion, Buddha recalls how he once felt so "hemmed in" by his followers that he found himself "in discomfort and not at ease." So after taking lunch, he tidied his lodgings and "without informing his attendant or taking leave of the order of monks, he set off alone, without a companion." Then he settled in a forest at the foot of a *sal* tree. Not only does he encourage his followers to find their own way in the world, when their company becomes overbearing, he slips off into the woods to escape the pressures of communal life. "To become independent of others" was considered by Buddha to be a characteristic of the person who has gained firsthand understanding of the dharma and thereby entered the path.

Over time, this model of autonomous self-reliance largely gave way to settled monastic institutions. But Buddha's own preference was clear. He urged his followers to disperse rather than congregate. Communal life was a useful expedient for training and periodic reflection, but only as long as it strengthened each individual's capacity to be fully in the world but not of it. The responsibility of the itinerant monk was twofold: to realize nirvana in the still depths of his own solitude and to foster a culture of awakening through his interactions with others.

No matter how many safeguards Buddha put in place to prevent it, nothing seems able to resist life's diabolic drift toward structures that enclose and limit. What starts out as a liberating vision risks mutating into an ideological force for preserving a status quo or securing the interests of an elite. Therapeutic practices harden into foolproof techniques; loose-knit communities ossify into oppressive institutions. The difference between idea and ideology, practice and technique, community and institution is blurred and organic. The former slide imperceptibly into the latter. In the ideas, practices, and precepts taught by Buddha lie the seeds of subsequent Buddhist ideologies, technologies, and institutions. These enclosing structures start to crystallize whenever a configuration of ideas, practices, and ways of life reaches a critical mass of size and power. They seem as much due to the systemic perversity of samsara as the conscious intentions of any one individual to contrive them.

When Buddha was seventy-two years old, his Judas-like cousin Devadatta rebelled against his authority and attempted to take control of the community of monks. In the figure of Devadatta, Mara becomes incarnate as the ideological and institutional shadow of Buddhism. Having spent the past forty-three years taunting Buddha from within, Mara now tries to destroy him from without.

Having failed to persuade Buddha to retire on grounds of age and hand control of the community over to him, Devadatta ordered his follower King Ajatasattu to "send some men to take the monk Gotama's life." When this attempt failed, Devadatta took it upon himself to murder his cousin. He climbed to the top of Vulture's Peak outside Rajagaha (Rajgir), in whose shade Buddha was walking alone, and hurled a boulder over the edge. Although the rock was deflected, a splinter broke off and struck Buddha's foot, drawing blood and causing "bodily feelings that were painful, sharp, racking, piercing, harrowing, disagreeable."

Buddha spread out his robe and lay on the ground to recover from his injuries. Immediately, "Mara came to him and addressed him in verse":

> *Do you lie down in a daze or drunk on poetry?*
> *Don't you have sufficient goals to meet?*
> *Alone in your secluded dwelling place*
> *Why do you dream away intent on sleep?*

This mocking voice of self-doubt seeks further to torment an old man whose life's work is in danger of being usurped and corrupted by someone whom he had earlier dismissed as "a wastrel, a clot of spittle." But Gotama neither "lies awake in dread" nor is "afraid to sleep." "Having reached the goal," he answers Mara, "I lie down out of compassion for beings." Mara vanished at once.

Devadatta now conspired to create a schism in the community of monks. He demanded that the monastic rule be reformed to accord more strictly with Buddha's emphasis on detachment and simplicity. Henceforth, he proposed, monks should only live in forests at the feet of trees, only eat alms they have begged for, only wear discarded rags, and only eat vegetarian food. As Devadatta expected, Buddha rejected the proposal on the grounds that monks should be at liberty to choose where they live and whether or not to accept offerings from householders. And as long as the animal was not killed for them personally, they were free to eat meat and fish. Presenting himself as the exemplary renunciant, Devadatta made it known that he would undertake to live by his proposed rules even if Buddha did not. Many younger monks voted to follow his example and left the community with him.

"For where God built a church," remarked Martin Luther two thousand years later, "there the devil would also build a chapel. . . . In such sort is the devil always God's ape." Or as Samuel Taylor Coleridge put it in his poem "The Devil's Thoughts,"

> *And the devil did grin, for his darling sin*
> *Is pride that apes humility.*

Buddha likewise compared Devadatta to a young calf elephant who imitates the old tusker's habit of eating lotus stalks but fails to wash them properly, falls ill, and dies. "Through aping me," said Buddha, Devadatta "will die wretchedly." On hearing that his idealistic young followers had been persuaded to change their minds and return to Buddha's fold, "then and there hot blood gushed from Devadatta's mouth." Although his rebellion failed, it was an ominous sign of the power struggles and ideological disputes that would bedevil Buddhism after Gotama's death.

Devadatta wanted to control Buddhism by enclosing it within tighter limits. He did not dispute the truth of the dharma, but sought to replace Buddha's liberal guidance with his own autocratic leadership. When Devadatta asked to be put in charge of the community of monks, Buddha did not refuse him because he had someone better qualified in mind. He refused because he had no intention that anyone should lead the community after his death. The dharma alone, he said, would suffice as one's guide. Each practitioner should be independent, "like an island." In rejecting Devadatta's reformed rule, Buddha did not disapprove of the practices themselves but of the restrictions the rule would have placed on the monks' liberty and social mobility.

In breaking with the Indian system of caste, Buddha freed his followers from the tyranny of a social order founded on the contingencies of birth. By creating an order of nuns, he liberated women from the tyranny of domestic servitude. In resisting Devadatta, he protected his community against the tyranny of repressive and autocratic leadership. In his conquest of Mara, he gained victory over the tyrannies of compulsion and biology. The common thread that unites these social, gendered, communal, and spiritual dimensions of life was Buddha's commitment to freedom. The task of a contemporary culture of awakening is not to imitate an historical religious form but to practice and extend these liberties while safeguarding them against the threat of their respective tyrannies.

Buddha compared the ideas and practices he taught to a raft

made of "grass, twigs, branches and leaves" tied together "for the purpose of crossing over, not for the purpose of grasping." Once the raft has enabled one to cross that "great expanse of water, whose near shore is dangerous and fearful and whose further shore is safe and free from fear," then it should be discarded. Otherwise it risks crystallizing into a sanctified version of the repetitive, restrictive, and frustrating behavior one seeks to overcome. One settles into comfortable spiritual routines, becomes fixated with correct interpretations of doctrine, and judges with self-righteous indignation anyone who corrupts the purity of the tradition.

The metaphor of the raft highlights the pragmatic and therapeutic nature of what Buddha taught. Rather than preaching an ideology, Gotama presented a range of ideas to be examined, tested, and applied in the light of experience. Instead of a calibrated sequence of spiritual techniques leading inexorably from one stage of the path to the next, he offered a range of practices suited to the lifestyles, temperaments, and predispositions of his audience. Rather than establish monastic institutions, he created a homeless community of renunciants, where each individual was encouraged to wander forth on his own for the welfare of others.

Over the centuries, Buddhism has repeatedly veered away from this founding vision. As with Christianity, a pattern of institutionalization recurred each time it became an established religion in a new land. For to succeed as a power in the world, a church needs to maintain an internally consistent ideology that grounds its institutions and hierarchies in infallible claims to truth. It has to insist on the efficacy of a precise spiritual technology in order to assure its followers that it can lead them step by step from despair to salvation. It requires elaborate lineages that can trace the authority of its priests through an unbroken succession back to the historical founder.

Institutions survive by repeating doctrines and techniques irrespective of whatever else is changing around them. A tradition will nonetheless survive the collapse of its institutions if it persists as a living community of practices and ideas. History has borne witness to the rise and fall of numerous Buddhist churches, each with its own distinctive ideology and techniques. Yet the tradition has managed to survive as a culture of awakening. Each time it has had to adapt to an unprecedented situation, this has stimulated a creative reimagining of itself. But once established in the new environment, a culture of awakening will tend toward stable and predictable patterns. This diabolic drift to ideologically based institutions is, to paraphrase Max Weber, the routinization of awakening.

Now that the Buddhist traditions of premodern Asia find themselves face to face with the liberal traditions of modernity, each challenges the other to look afresh at its understanding and practice of freedom. Just as Buddhism provides psychological insights and contemplative practices to free people from their inner demons, so the liberal philosophies of

Europe and America provide social insights and political practices to free people from governments and religions that restrict their liberty to live as they choose. We thus come to appreciate the full extent of Mara's reach: intense private hatreds share with complex societal structures of repression the same capacity to block paths and limit freedom.

21

The Kingdom of Mara

NOT ONLY DID BUDDHA have to contend with rebellions within his own community, to achieve his goals he had to operate within a world of social change and political upheaval. In the prosperous Gangetic basin of North India, power was shifting from republican confederacies of clans to autocratic monarchies with imperial ambitions. Contrary to legend, Gotama was not a prince of even a minor kingdom but the son of a leading elder within the oligarchic republic of Shakya. Although he had renounced his own role as a political leader upon becoming a wandering ascetic, after his awakening he required the patronage and protection of the political powers of his time in order that his community and teachings could survive.

He found much of this patronage and protection where wealth and power were most concentrated: in the kingdoms of

Magadha and Kosala. His major training and teaching centers were duly established in Rajagaha, capital of Magadha, and Savatthi (Sravasti), capital of Kosala. To a lesser extent, he stayed and taught at Vesali, capital of the Vajjian Confederacy, the largest surviving republic. As Gotama's prestige grew and his order of monks expanded, his fate became unavoidably tied to the political ambitions and fortunes of these states.

His first major patron was King Bimbisara of Magadha. Bimbisara is presented as a powerful but humane ruler, who from an early age had aspired both to kingship and spiritual insight. Not long after the awakening, Buddha traveled with his followers to Rajagaha. On hearing his teaching, the king "penetrated the dharma, left uncertainty behind him, his doubts vanished, he acquired perfect confidence and became independent of others." In gratitude, this now enlightened monarch offered Gotama a park on the edge of town called the Bamboo Grove, where the monks could train and practice.

Bimbisara appears to have continued ruling wisely for the next thirty years, but little more is heard of him until Devadatta mounts his rebellion. After Buddha refused Devadatta's request to lead the community of monks, Devadatta went to his disciple Prince Ajatasattu, Bimbisara's heir, and said, "Formerly, men were long-lived, now they are short-lived. Maybe you will die while still only a prince. So why do you not kill your father and become king? And I shall kill Gotama and become Buddha." Ajatasattu "fastened a dagger on his thigh" and slipped into the king's private quarters. But he raised suspicion among the guards and was arrested. The dagger was found and the plot exposed. When the prince was brought to his father, the king asked why he wanted to kill him. "I want the kingdom, sir," replied the prince. "If you want the kingdom," said the king, "the kingdom is yours."

Thus Ajatasattu became king of Magadha. To secure his power, he murdered his father anyway. He starved the old man to death in prison, which caused his mother, Kosaladevi, to die of grief. As a parricide, Ajatasattu was a killer (Mara) with whom Buddha had to contend in order that his community might survive in Magadha. Their next encounter was arranged by the royal physician. As Ajatasattu approached the grove where Buddha was staying, he "felt fear and terror and his hair stood on end." But after hearing Buddha speak about the fruits of the homeless life, he was so inspired that he formally became a follower and confessed to murdering his father. "Since you have acknowledged the transgression and confessed it," says Buddha, "I will accept it. For one who so confesses will grow in the noble life."

Rather than chastise him for murder, Buddha forgives him. "Rejoicing and delighting" at Buddha's words, Ajatasattu devoutly takes his leave and departs. But as soon as the king is out of sight, Buddha turns to his monks and says, "The king is done for, his fate is sealed! If he had not deprived his father of his life, then as he sat here the pure vision of dharma would have arisen in him." Buddha seems to be saying one thing to Ajatasattu and another to his monks. Having given the king hope and encouragement in the noble life, he then declares how his crime deprived him of the chance of realizing the noble life.

Buddha's other major patron was King Pasenadi, ruler of Kosala, the powerful monarchy that bordered on Buddha's homeland of Shakya. Kosala was allied to Magadha through marriage. Pasenadi's sister Kosaladevi was Bimbisara's wife and Ajatasattu's mother. Buddha was an exact contemporary of Pasenadi and spent twenty-four monsoons at the Jetavana Grove in the Kosalan capital of Savatthi, where he delivered a great deal of his teaching.

Several discourses recount Buddha's exchanges with Pasenadi. Unlike his brother-in-law Bimbisara, Pasenadi shows little interest in awakening. He admits that he is typical of those kings "who are intoxicated with sovereignty, obsessed by greed for sensual pleasures, have obtained stable control in their country, and rule having conquered a great sphere of territory on earth." Although the two men knew each other well, instead of advising or admonishing the king on specific issues, Buddha tends just to offer him broad themes for reflection.

On hearing of Pasenadi's battles with Ajatasattu (a dispute over a village that was part of Kosaladevi's dowry to Bimbisara), Buddha does not criticize Pasenadi for engaging in warfare and makes no attempt to persuade him to turn Kosala into a peaceful, nonviolent state. Nor does Buddha disapprove of the king disguising his spies and undercover agents as wandering ascetics. Instead, he draws the moral that one should not judge people by their outward appearance alone. On learning that a great animal sacrifice is being prepared by the king, Buddha criticizes this practice to his monks but makes no effort to prevent it from taking place. And when Pasenadi arrests "a great mass of people" and binds them with ropes and chains, Buddha points out how much stronger are the bonds of "infatuation with jewelry and earrings" and "anxious concern for wives and children."

As a warlord, sensualist, deceiver, and tyrant, Pasenadi possesses the key features of Mara. It is probably no accident that Buddha's discussions with this king immediately precede his dialogues with Mara in the Pali Canon. Although Pasenadi is presented as a lay follower of Buddha, unlike Bimbisara he is not recorded as attaining any spiritual insight. The only time his behavior is seen to be changed by Buddha's advice is when he agrees to eat less in order to lose weight. Even after the king has just impaled a band of rebels, Buddha does not chastise him. He reminds him that "when ageing and death are rolling in on you, great king," no amount of arms or wealth can stand in their way. There is nothing to be done "but to live by the dharma, live righteously, and do wholesome and meritorious deeds."

In contrast to Buddha's sardonic manner with Mara, his attitude to Ajatasattu and Pasenadi appears circumspect and cautious. As ruthless autocrats who control a world in which Gotama is historically and socially enmeshed, these kings have a hold over Buddha that Mara lacks. Even the Pali commentarial tradition, which aims to present Buddha in the best possible light, has him think (after the impaling episode with Pasenadi): "If I reprimand [the king] for such a terrible deed, he will feel too dismayed to associate closely with me. Instead I will instruct him by an indirect method." Such sentiments acknowledge how Buddha cannot ignore the pressures of the political reality in which he lives and plays a role.

The final meeting between Pasenadi and Buddha takes place in Shakya when both men are eighty years old. Having elaborately praised Buddha and his monks, the king concludes ominously, "And now we depart. We are busy and have much to do." When the king takes leave of Buddha, he is informed that the general with whom he had come to Shakya has departed with the royal insignia and crowned Pasenadi's son Vidudabha as king. Isolated, Pasenadi hurries to Magadha to summon the help of his nephew and erstwhile enemy Ajatasattu. But the gates of Rajagaha are closed. Weary from the journey, he collapses outside the city walls and dies.

Then Buddha travels south to Magadha and stays at his retreat on Vulture's Peak outside the capital. While there, Ajatasattu informs him that he intends to attack the Vajjian Confederacy, the last republican stronghold in northern India on the northern border of Magadha. Buddha leaves Rajagaha and heads back toward his homeland by way of Vesali, the Vajjian capital, on what will be his last journey. It is unclear what prompts this move. At some point, he may have learned that

Vidudabha (Pasenadi's son) had invaded the Shakyan republic in revenge for the dishonor of being the son of a slave-girl given in marriage to his father under the pretense of being a Shakyan noblewoman. It is said that Buddha tried three times in vain to persuade him to withdraw. Adhering to the precept against killing, the Shakyans offered only symbolic resistance and were massacred by Vidudabha's troops. The Shakyan territory was then incorporated into Kosala.

Around the same time, Buddha, who had already fallen ill at Vesali, succumbs to food-poisoning and dies in Kusinara, described by his attendant Ananda as a "miserable little wattle-and-daub town, right in the jungle in the back of beyond." From his broader (and, one suspects, ironic) perspective, Buddha criticizes Ananda for talking this way. Long ago, he said, Kusinara was the city of Kusavati, which was "rich and prosperous, crowded with people and well-stocked with food. It was never free of the sound of elephants, horses, carriages, drums, lutes, singing, cymbals, with cries of 'Eat, drink, and be merry!'" Such is the fate of cities and civilizations. No matter how powerful they become, their glory will fade and be forgotten.

The world around Buddha was torn apart. The political forces that had until then been held in check erupted in a storm of destruction. Not only did Vidudabha exterminate the Shakyans, Ajatasattu then conquered the Vajjian Confederacy, thus wiping out the only significant republican state in the region. Was the circumspection Buddha exhibited in his discussions with Ajatasattu and Pasenadi diplomatically motivated to preserve the delicate balance of power between these contending states? Whether or not he intentionally played a political role, Gotama had to function within a world every bit as devious, violent, and unpredictable as our own.

In their last conversation, Pasenadi says to Buddha, "I am a Kosalan and you are a Kosalan." Buddha does not deny this. By the end of his life, he had come to regard himself as a subject of the king. In accepting the protection of the Kosalan state, he tacitly acknowledges the state's willingness to use violence to protect the rights and freedoms of its subjects should the territorial integrity and peace of the realm be threatened. This too would explain his reluctance to criticize the king for his violent behavior.

To tackle Mara in the political realm is a hazardous exercise that calls for utmost vigilance and care. Gotama had to realize his goals within the political environment of his time, but his goals were not in themselves political. Shortly after the awakening, before Brahma had inspired him to set off into the world, two merchants offered him some rich food that made him ill and weak. Mara appeared and urged him not to fight the sickness but die. "I shall not enter final nirvana," retorted Buddha, "until my disciples have become learned, wise, and intelligent, . . . sufficiently accomplished in their own discourse so that my teaching will be extensively practiced and spread far and wide among many people." Fifty years later,

with his world collapsing around him and his body succumbing to illness and age, he had succeeded in accomplishing this
goal and could die without regrets. And while his footprints
still leave their mark today, the traces of Bimbisara, Ajatasattu,
and Pasenadi survive as mere footnotes to his story.

22

Hearing the Cries

IN 494 BCE, around the time Buddha was dealing with the rebellions of Devadatta and Ajatasattu in north India, the consul Menenius Agrippa successfully put down a slave revolt in Rome. Agrippa persuaded the slaves that just as it would be unreasonable for the limbs of a body to rebel against the belly that sustains them, so it was unreasonable for workers to rebel against the Senate. Convinced, the slaves left their entrenched positions on the Aventine Hill and returned to the city to serve their masters. The same argument has also been used to justify the Indian caste system, in which each caste is seen as a different body part of the great primordial Man (*Purusha*): "His mouth became the Brahmin; his arms were made into the Warrior, his thighs the People, and from his feet the Servants were born." By sacrificing narrow self-interest and acting according to one's nature, each person thereby plays an essential role in sustaining the greater life of the whole.

When Shantideva uses this same organicist metaphor to illustrate how all beings are empathetically interconnected, and Pascal and Eckhart, following Paul, draw on it to affirm how all members of the church are one in the body of Christ, they ignore its potential for justifying tyranny. The story of Agrippa shows how the mere recognition of the organic interconnectedness of society is not in itself sufficient to generate compassion for others. Nor does the Indian belief that all people are one as members of a single body imply that they are entitled to the same rights or freedoms. For although the brain and a toe are interconnected parts of the same whole, this does not accord them equal significance. The organism can continue to function without a toe but not without a brain. One part is dispensable, while the other is not.

In the light of modern biology, an animal's body is not only a complex self-regulating organism but also a killing field. Hundreds of millions of bacterial cells live in your saliva, and countless numbers are wiped out each time you spit or brush your teeth. About a million more live on the surface of each square inch of skin, only to die each time you take a hot, soapy shower. The immune system is designed to both trap and expel microorganisms before they gain entry to the body, as well as to identify and destroy those that manage to penetrate the first layer of defense. As food is broken down and digested, the intestinal walls and floor become factories of death. Your very survival entails the systematic, ongoing destruction of millions of living things.

An organicist conception of life is entirely compatible with violent, autocratic, hierarchical, and undemocratic models of society. It has been appealed to by fascist states to justify the natural urge of the strong and healthy to overcome the weak and powerless. In comparing a criminal to a diseased finger that must be amputated before it infects the rest of the body, Chinese Communists have used it to justify the death penalty. In each case, the metaphor is employed to legitimate the oppression of one section of society by another. A political or religious elite is able to secure its privileges by persuading others that they are destined by nature to play a subordinate and submissive role.

To understand the way something *is* does not enable us to conclude how we *should* then act. Even if we *are* profoundly interconnected in the complex web of life, as Shantideva and others suggest, this need not imply that we *should* love each other as equals or treat one another with tolerance and respect. How we interpret and use this metaphor will depend on the kind of worldview, values, and principles that we already honor and seek to uphold. Insight into the interconnectedness of life will only reinforce feelings of universal love and respect if we are already committed to the principles of equality, liberty, compassion, and nonviolence.

The image of life as a single organism in which we are all

connected to each other is an insufficient basis for morality and ethics. To respond to the other's suffering as though it were my own requires more than just knowing that the other is part of a greater whole that unites us. I need to hear the other's call not to hurt her in such a way that I hear in it the echo of my own call for her not to hurt me. No matter how reasonably I can define her as friend, foe, or stranger, I have to discard this limited picture in order to encounter the other as a contingent, fragile creature who silently cries out not to be hurt. This requires suspending preconceived notions of the other and refining a capacity to listen.

Meditative awareness is more akin to hearing well than seeing clearly. When looking intently at a visual object, we tend to aim a narrow beam of attention onto something outside of ourselves. But when we listen mindfully, we open our awareness in all directions in order to receive the sounds that pour in. Just as one develops a meditative ability to discern ever subtler tones and harmonies in this polyphony, so one can refine an empathetic ability to detect ever finer nuances in the other's plea. As the deafening chatter of self-centeredness subsides, one recovers that silence wherein one hears more sharply the cries of the world.

In the Chinese *Surangama Sutra,* Gotama asks his assembled disciples about the most effective way to awaken. Avalokiteshvara, the bodhisattva who personifies Buddha's compassion, replies that using "the organ of hearing to quiet the mind for its entry into the stream of meditation" is the best method. In

China, the male figure of Avalokiteshvara mutated into the female bodhisattva Kuan-yin, whose name means "Observer of Sounds." Kuan-yin embodies a maternal compassion that is a response to the call of the other not to be hurt. Her graceful repose suggests how contemplative listening grounds and nurtures the open-hearted empathy that risks responding to the other's call.

To respond to the other's call in this way is the origin of nonviolence. Such nonviolence is not equivalent to mere passivity in the face of opposition. In confronting someone's rage, the wisest course of action may be to say and do nothing. But it might be to stand one's ground, speak out firmly, even resist the aggression physically. It depends on how one assesses the degree of harm the aggressor is liable to inflict. As a moral principle, nonviolence is an unambiguous commitment to respond to others' call not to hurt them. As a moral practice, requiring at times instant decisions based on inadequate knowledge, it is to risk saying or doing something that will have consequences we cannot foresee and may not intend.

People want to live in communities and societies that honor and protect the inviolability of the space each person cherishes as his or her own. This space is respected not because it encloses an immutable soul but because it is the unobstructed openness that can become a selfless person's path. For this is the space one cultivates by paying mindful attention to the flux of embodied experience, thereby eroding the conviction that a tight cell of "me" endures somewhere at its core. Since this emptiness *is* the path, to intrude into another's life in a way that violates that space is tantamount to blocking her path.

The only grounds an individual or a society has to block a person's path is if that path inflicts, or threatens to inflict, harm on that person as well as others. While Buddha regarded the freedom of nirvana as the "ground" and "goal" of life, the experience of that freedom heightened his awareness of the call of others not to be hurt. During his lifetime, Gotama established a community (sangha) committed to this principle of nonviolent freedom to serve as a model of a nonviolent and free society. Each generation since has had to face the double challenge of maintaining the sangha while transforming the wider society around it in the light of its values.

The most far-reaching transformations of human society in recent times have come, however, not from the Buddhist East but from the sociopolitical movements of the Christian West that gained an irresistible momentum with the independence of the United States in 1783 and the French Revolution of 1789. *The Declaration of the Rights of Man and Citizens,* approved in Paris on August 26, 1789, likewise affirms the centrality of nonviolent freedom. Its fourth article states:

> Freedom consists in being able to do whatever does not harm the other: thus the exercise of the natural rights of man has as its only limits those that assure other members of society the enjoyment of the same rights.

Each person is free to lead whatever life he chooses provided it does not violate the freedom of others to do likewise. Unless a person's actions harm others, no one has the right to prevent him from following that course. This notion of personal freedom and rights is so embedded in modern liberal democracies that it appears to us as little more than common sense. It seems so self-evident that we may only become conscious of it when it is threatened.

Most traditional forms of Buddhism, by contrast, bear the imprint of monarchic and aristocratic societies of the kind overthrown by the American and French revolutions. The transformation of Indian society into a casteless meritocracy of self-creating and self-transcending persons envisioned by Buddha failed to materialize. The system of caste and the power of kings prevailed, and Buddhism died out, prompting many former Buddhists to convert to Islam as a way of preserving their caste-free status. Elsewhere in Asia, Buddhism tended to ally itself with powerful aristocratic patrons, thereby limiting its capacity for initiating radical social change. The detachment of monastic institutions, an inherited wariness of secular politics, and a growing bias toward introspection all contributed to Buddhism's preference for gently modifying a status quo rather than seeking to overthrow it.

The liberal democracies of modernity unintentionally realize certain aspects of the kind of society envisioned by Buddha. As the son of a leading elder within the republic of Shakya, Gotama spoke approvingly of the nonautocratic, consultative approach to government, which was best exemplified at his time in the Vajjian Confederacy, and used it as a model for organizing his monastic order. The structure of the sangha reflected republican rather than monarchic values.

Likewise, in rejecting the notion of caste, Buddha abandoned the idea that a person's identity or destiny is determined by nature. He declared:

> No one is born a brahmin. A brahmin is a brahmin because of what he *does* . . . A farmer is a farmer because of what he does and a craftsman a craftsman because of what he does. A merchant, a servant, a thief, a soldier, a priest or a king: each of them is what he is because of what he does.

This performative conception of self entails each individual's freedom to pursue the form of life he or she selects. The self is thus neither nonexistent nor eternal but created by one's acts. A society composed of members who define their own roles within it while respecting the rights of others to do likewise is an open and tolerant one.

Despite his republican instincts, Gotama did not abandon the idea of nobility. He redefined it as the inherent dignity of a person creating a path to awakening. He called his four truths "ennobling": to understand anguish, let go of craving, embark on a path, and glimpse nirvana enhance the dignity of the person. Buddha saw that even a killer such as Angulimala possessed the glimmerings of such dignity as well as the capacity to rise above his limitations and break free of Mara's grip. As would become more explicit as Buddhists worked out the implications of Gotama's vision, all sentient beings possess the inviolable dignity of their buddhanature.

The creation of a nonviolent world is founded on an empathetic respect for the inviolable freedoms and rights of others. The oppressed call out to be free to pursue a path, unconstrained by the constraints placed on them by Mara's latter-day army of governments, religions, superpowers, and market forces. Now that the principalities and the powers stockpile weapons of mass destruction, contaminate the earth with their feverish industry, release floods of images to trigger insatiable desires, treat animals and humans as commodities and functions of a market, the devil must be grinning from ear to ear. As sovereign nation-states behave more and more like personalities (embodied and caricatured in the figure of monarchs, presidents, and dictators), they assume the diabolic features of a disconnected cell of self, blind to their own defects and infatuated by their own image.

The devil is incarnate today as the structural violence that pervades and ruptures the interconnected world. To demonize parts of this global network as evil while glorifying others as good is to succumb to Mara's dualistic urge to split things apart. Instead of recognizing how good and evil, God and Satan, Buddha and Mara are inseparable from each other, we divide them into two fundamentally opposed powers. Ignoring what history has repeatedly and bloodily taught, we persist in destroying what we perceive as evil in the hope that one day only good (i.e., ourselves and whatever values we hold) will prevail. Only now much more is at stake than before. The earth has become too small and our capacity for destruction too immense to sustain this kind of conflict forever.

23

The Anarchy of the Gaps

BUDDHA AND MARA ARE figurative ways of portraying a fundamental opposition within human nature. While "Buddha" stands for a capacity for awareness, openness, and freedom, "Mara" represents a capacity for confusion, closure, and restriction. To live with the devil is to live with the perpetual conflict between one's buddhanature and one's maranature. When buddhanature prevails, fixations ease and the world brightens, revealing itself as empty, contingent, and fluid. When maranature dominates, fixations tighten and the world appears opaque, necessary, static. William Blake evokes a similar opposition in *The Marriage of Heaven and Hell* (begun in 1789, the year of the French Revolution): "If the doors of perception were cleansed, every thing would appear to man as it is: Infinite. For man has closed himself up, till he sees all things thro' narrow chinks of his cavern."

Buddhanature and maranature are inseparable from each other. Like a valve that can either be open or closed, this organism has the capacity to unfold (buddha) or shut down (mara). The Sanskrit term translated as "nature" is *garbha,* which means "womb." Buddhanature is like the empty, warm, fertile space from which I was born. My womblike nature suggests that I am not the necessary, static self I feel myself to be, but a contingent creature with an extraordinary but often untapped capacity for growth and change. My maranature, however, is that side of me that compulsively resists such transformation, refuses to be touched and impregnated with any ideas other than its own certainties, and stubbornly clings to the illusion of being a frozen and isolate self.

Or think of it like this: "buddhanature" stands for that open perspective whence one is free to respond to the call of others; "maranature" stands for those fixed positions that prompt one to react. While a perspective allows the possibility of pursuing a path into an unknown, a position ensures that you never stray from the territory you have already staked out. Designating that territory as "Buddhist" or "postmodern" does not prevent it from becoming another stronghold of Mara. What was once a perspective can crystallize into a position. Convinced that you were moving ahead, you find that you have only traced another circle.

Buddha's perspective is conveyed by the Pali term *appamada,* which can be translated as "care." In the *Dhammapada,* Buddha describes this vigilant care as "the path to the deathless." "The careful do not die," he adds, whereas "the careless are like the dead." By identifying care with the path and opposing it to death, he locates it at the heart of the struggle with Mara. His last words as he lay dying in Kusinara were, "Conditions are subject to decay. Work out your salvation with care."

As the perspective of one pursuing a path, care is an existential sensibility rather than a discrete mental act. Buddhist analyses of care describe it as a configuration of different interwoven elements. Such care is grounded in an energetic state of contentment, kindness, and clarity. When this careful caring is activated, greed, hatred, and confusion are (for the time being) suspended. The twelfth-century Tibetan lama Thogmé Zangpo defined care as "a keen concern for engagement and letting go." Care is that which cherishes and cultivates virtues while also relinquishing compulsive behavior. As an awareness of one's values and a diligent commitment to realize them, it deprives Mara of a foothold, thereby guarding one against his attacks.

Such a path of vigilant care is not an exclusively Buddhist concern. Whatever sheds light on impermanence, suffering, contingency, and emptiness can contribute to a path that inclines toward nirvana, even if it originates in a secular tradition that is skeptical of religion, or in a religion that denies the validity of Buddhism. In recognizing the existence of "solitary buddhas" (*paccekabuddha*), who gain insight into the nature of contingency independently of a teacher or Buddhist community, Buddhism affirms that the attainment of nirvana can occur outside of a Buddhist context. Job and Jesus, Pascal and Montaigne, evolutionary biology and neuroscience, Roland Barthes and William Blake offer glimpses of self and world that illuminate the path opened up by Buddha.

Although a devout Buddhist, Shantideva aspires "always to be a student of everyone, respectfully accepting unsolicited words which are of help, openly rejoicing in whatever is well said." To enclose oneself in the confines of a tradition and community where one feels at home and unthreatened cuts one off from the myriad sources of awakening that are everywhere present, were one only prepared to reach out and embrace them. "There is nothing whatsoever," affirms Shantideva, "that is not to be learned by one who aspires to awaken."

In such encounters between traditions are the seeds of a contemporary culture of awakening likely to germinate. This culture might already be fermenting in the dialogues and exchanges between declared Buddhists and "solitary buddhas" who, unbeknown to themselves, are gouging pathways to nirvana. It can embrace both secular and religious elements while in itself being neither secular nor religious. Yet a culture of awakening does not rest on the universalist assumption that all "spiritual" paths ultimately lead to the same destination: some may be vicious circles that go nowhere, while others may be in thrall to longings for eternity. As a middle way, such a culture would be rooted in a vigilant care that is constantly on guard against the lures of both the demonic and divine.

At a time when the all-embracing certainties of closed societies and belief systems no longer convince or reassure us, more and more do we find ourselves in that perplexing middle ground *between* communities and ideas. Having embraced this homelessness, we are at liberty to weave our way between Buddhism and monotheism, the religious and the secular, science and art, literature and myth. In exploring the fertile spaces between traditions, we open up a path that may be rooted in a specific tradition but has branched out into the no-man's-land between them all.

In an open society saturated with information, the gaps between traditions serve as a refreshing but unsettling wilderness. By dwelling in their emptiness, we are able to return to those questions for which each tradition claims to have the answers. The anarchy of the gaps makes it impossible for any ideology or religion to take hold. For the very act of laying claim to that inbetween space would enclose it in boundaries and compromise its openness, thereby turning it into a closed space separated from other closed spaces, thus creating more gaps that are beyond one's reach.

To wander along the gaps allows the freedom to ask anew the questions posed by being born and having to die. Humans like ourselves may never have evolved before and may never evolve again in this or any other universe. As far as anyone knows, we are alone in an inconceivably vast cosmos that has no interest at all in our fate. Even if other worlds like this exist elsewhere in the cosmos, they would not be mere repetitions of the awesomely complex configuration of biological, cultural, and psychological conditions that are generating this world now. The path that has led you here and beckons you into an unknown future has likewise never appeared in exactly this way before and will not do so again. You are free to go straight ahead, turn right, or turn left. Nothing is stopping you. Having gained knowledge of good and evil through eating forbidden fruit, Adam and Eve were exposed to the anguish and exhilaration of making such choices. "The world was all before them," says Milton in describing their departure from paradise, while

> They hand in hand with wand'ring steps and slow,
> Through Eden took their solitary way.

NOTES

Throughout this book, I have used Pali spellings of Buddhist terms, the only exceptions being Sanskrit words already incorporated into the English language, e.g., karma, nirvana, dharma. All quoted passages from Baudelaire, Pascal, and Barthes are my own translations from the French. The following classical Buddhist texts are referred to in the notes by these abbreviations:

BCA Shantideva. *The Bodhicaryavatara: A Guide to the Bodhisattva's Way of Life*. Each verse newly translated from Tibetan by the author. Chapter number, followed by verse number.

DN Buddha. *Digha Nikaya: The Long Discourses of the Buddha*. Translated by Maurice Walshe. Discourse number, followed by section number, followed by page number of English translation.

LC Lin-chi. *The Record of Lin-chi*. Ruth Fuller Sazaki, translator. Kyoto: Institute for Zen Studies, 1975.

Notes

MMK Nagarjuna. *Mulamadhyamakakarika: The Fundamental Wisdom of the Middle Way.* Each verse newly translated from Tibetan by the author. Chapter number, followed by verse number.

MN Buddha. *Majjhima Nikaya: The Middle Length Discourses of the Buddha.* Translated by Bhikkhu Nanamoli and Bhikkhu Bodhi. Discourse number, followed by section number, followed by page number of English translation.

SN Buddha. *Samyutta Nikaya: The Connected Discourses of the Buddha.* Translated by Bhikkhu Bodhi. Part number, followed by section number, followed by discourse number, followed by page number of English translation.

Sn Buddha. *The Sutta-Nipata.* Translated by H. Saddhatissa. Chapter number, followed by discourse number, followed by verse number, followed by page number of English translation.

Epigraph

p. xi "I do not know who put me in the world": Pascal, *Pensées,* no. 398, p. 256–7 (English: no. 427, p. 158).

ONE: THE GOD OF THIS AGE

1. Parallel Mythologies

p. 7 "the abode of a great person": MN 151.2, p. 1143.

p. 7 "Buddhas say emptiness": MMK 13.8.

p. 9 "self-begot, self-raised / By our own quick'ning power": Milton, *Paradise Lost,* Book V, lines 860–1.

2. This Need Not Have Happened

p. 13 Or had the policeman's gun that fired the bullet: Kershaw, *Hitler: 1889–1936: Hubris,* Vol. I, p. 211.

p. 15 When Dante enters hell's ninth and final circle: Dante, *Divine Comedy, Inferno,* Canto 34.

p. 15 "the king of the vast kingdom of all grief": Ibid., line 28.

p. 16 "I yearn to be free of pain": BCA 1.28.

p. 16 "we desire truth and find in ourselves nothing but uncertainty": Pascal, *Pensées,* no. 380, p. 240 (English: no. 401, p. 398).

3. Mara—The Killer

p. 18 "I was living on the bank of the Neranjara River": Sn 3.2.425–8, p. 48. *The Striving (Padhana Sutta)* is one of the texts collected in the *Sutta-Nipata.*

p. 18 "I see your troops all around me": Sn 3.2.442–3, p. 49.

p. 18 "any power so hard to conquer": DN 26.28, p. 405.

p. 19 He enumerates the armies: Sn 3.2.436–8, pp. 48–9.

p. 19 "I remember once seeing a crow": Sn 3.2.447–8, p. 49.

p. 20 "whom Mara cannot overcome, any more than the winds": *Mahavastu,* II, 241; quoted in Boyd, *Satan and Mara,* p. 98.

p. 20 "has deprived Mara's eye of its opportunity . . . blindfolded Mara . . . invisible": MN 26.34, p. 267.

p. 20 "All those distortions, manoeuvres, and contortions": SN 1.4.24, p. 216.

p. 21 "It makes no difference what you grasp": Sn 5.12.1103, p. 127.

p. 21 "one who withholds the waters": Ling, *Buddhism and the Mythology of Evil,* p. 55.

p. 21 "I know you, evil one": This occurs, for example, as a refrain in MN 49.6, p. 425*ff.* seq. Alternately, as a refrain throughout SN 1.4, Mara acknowledges his failure to influence Buddha by saying, "The Blessed One knows me, the Fortunate One knows me."

p. 22 "Mara was so upset by his failure": Sn 3.2.449, p. 49.

p. 22 "Mara shook his head, lolled his tongue": SN 1.4.21, p. 211.

p. 22 "went away from that spot": SN 1.4.25, p. 217.

p. 22 "a farmer, carrying a large plough": SN 1.4.19, p. 208.

p. 22 "with a large matted topknot, clad in an antelope hide": SN 1.4.21, pp. 210–1.

p. 23 "The eyes are mine. Shapes and colors are mine": SN 1.4.19, p. 208.

p. 23 "Where there are no eyes, no shapes or colors": Ibid.

p. 23 "arouse fear, trepidation and terror": A refrain that occurs at the opening of several discourses in SN 1.4.

p. 23 "as though the earth were splitting open": SN 1.4.17, p. 206.

p. 23 He shatters boulders near Buddha, he appears as a giant elephant . . . : These appear, respectively, in SN 1.4.11, p. 202; SN 1.4.2, p. 196; SN 1.4.6, p. 199; SN 1.4.16, p. 205.

p. 24 *Mara* means "the killer": Cf. John 8.44—"Ye are of your father the devil, and the lusts of your father ye will do. He was a murderer from the beginning, and abode not in the truth, because there is no truth in him."

p. 24 "You have accomplished everything . . . You need not worry, evil one": DN 16.3.7, pp. 246, 247.

p. 24 Buddha calls Mara the *Antaka:* This epithet occurs repeatedly throughout SN 1.4; see, for example, SN 1.4.1, p. 196.

p. 25 "catch Buddha with the snare of lust": SN 1.4.25, p. 217. Mara's daughters are called Tanha, Arati, and Raga, which mean Craving, Discontent, and Lust.

p. 25 While Buddha remains alert to the urges of his biology: The text alludes to impotence metaphorically: "or else he would have dried up and withered away and become shriveled, just as a green reed that has been mowed down would dry up and wither away and become shriveled," ibid., p. 218.

p. 25 "the wind a fallen cotton tuft": Ibid., p. 220.

pp. 25–26 "Long is the life span of human beings . . . Short is the life span of human beings": SN 1.4.9, p. 201.

p. 26 Buddhism developed a theory of four maras: In Pali, these are, respectively: *khandha-mara, kilesa-mara, yama-mara,* and *devaputta-mara.* The fifth mara is *kamma-* or *abhisankhara-mara.*

p. 27 "A *picture* held us captive": Wittgenstein, *Philosophical Investigations,* 115, p. 48.

p. 28 Over the centuries, this culminated in Buddha's becoming impossibly perfect: In the discourses of Mahayana Buddhism, Buddha has become so perfect that Mara can no longer get near him. On the rare occasions when the devil appears, it is not as a disheveled farmer with muddy feet but as a remote personification of evil. The translator Conze, in *The Large Sutra on Perfect Wisdom,* describes Mara as preparing a fourfold army to attack Buddha (pp. 240–1). On becoming aware of the plot, a god in Buddha's retinue "called to mind the Perfection of Wisdom and repeated it in his memory. Immediately Mara turned back on his path." All it takes to get rid of Mara are a few thoughts turned over in the mind of a clairvoyant god.

4. Satan—The Adversary

p. 29 "command this stone that it be made bread": Luke 4.3 and Matthew 4.3.

p. 29 "he need only resolve that the Himalaya . . . exercise ruler-

ship righteously": SN 1.4.20, p. 210. It is striking that these two examples closely follow each other in the respective texts.

p. 30 "the Destroyer . . . the accursed destructive spirit": Cited in
Russell, *The Devil,* p. 108.

p. 30 "Zarathustra was the first to see in the struggle": Friedrich
Nietzsche, *Ecce Homo,* p. 127. Translated by R. J. Hollingdale. Harmondsworth and New York: Penguin, 1979.

p. 31 "No one is *born* a brahmin": Sn 3.9.650, p. 75.

p. 32 "From going to and fro in the earth": Job 1.7 and 2.2; 2.5;
2.7.

p. 32 "His troops come together": Job 19.12.

p. 32 *"Why is light given* to a man": Job 3.23.

pp. 32–33 "Mara Conquering Sage": Pali: *Marabhibumuni.* Sn 545,
p. 63; and 571, p. 67.

p. 33 "him that hath the power of death": Hebrews 2.14.

p. 33 "You are a human being": *Mahavastu,* II, 269; quoted in Boyd,
Satan and Mara, p. 114.

p. 33 "I am nobler than he. You created me from fire": Koran 7.11–
24 (other versions of this story appear in 2.32–7 and 15.26–37).

pp. 33–34 "Lord, since You have seduced me": Koran 15.33.

p. 34 "ruler of this world": John 12.31.

p. 34 "the god of this age": II Corinthians 4.4.

p. 34 "We are not contending against flesh and blood": Ephesians
6.12.

p. 34 "For the demonic is the elevation": Tillich, *Systematic Theology,*
I, p. 140; see also III, pp. 102*ff.*

p. 35 "must suffer many things, and be rejected": Mark 8.31; 8.33.

p. 35 "that old serpent, called the Devil": Revelation 12.9.

p. 35 "saw Satan fall like lightning": Luke 10.18.

p. 35 "fell bodily into the great hell of Avici": *Abhidharmakosa,* III, 41; quoted in Boyd, *Mara and Satan,* p. 115.

p. 36 "dwells five hundred miles": Gampopa, *Jewel Ornament of Liberation,* p. 62.

p. 36 "We know no time . . . when we were not as now": Milton, *Paradise Lost,* Book V, line 859*ff.*

p. 36 "perfect image": Ibid., Book II, lines 764, 795.

p. 36 "swim in mirth, and fancy": Ibid., Book IX, lines 1009–10; lines 1121–6.

p. 38 "this last enemy will not be its nonexistence": Quoted in Boyd, *Satan and Mara,* p. 60.

5. Boredom and Violence

p. 39 "yapping, yelling, groaning, creeping monsters": Baudelaire, *Les Fleurs du Mal,* "Au Lecteur."

pp. 40–41 "Stupidity, error, avarice, sin . . . A populace of Demons cavorts in our brain": Ibid.

p. 41 "Ceaselessly the Demon races at my side": Ibid. "Destruction" is the opening poem of the section entitled "Les Fleurs du Mal."

p. 42 "When we breathe, Death's invisible river": Ibid., "Au Lecteur."

p. 43 "We steal a secret pleasure on the side": Ibid.

p. 43 "Someone must have been telling lies about Joseph K.": Kafka, *The Trial,* p. 7.

p. 43 "a liar . . . a murderer from the beginning": John 8.44.

p. 43 "Suddenly, no, at last, long last": Beckett, *Stories and Texts for Nothing,* p. 75.

p. 44 "It seemed to me pleasant, and all the more agreeable": Baudelaire, *Les Fleurs du Mal,* p. 243.

p. 44 "So he leads me, far from God's sight": Ibid., "Destruction."

p. 45 "The undependable lord of death": BCA 2.33.

p. 46 "It is more difficult to love God": Baudelaire, *Les Fleurs du Mal,* p. 242.

Two: Creating a Path

6. Fear and Trembling

p. 51 "All the unhappiness of men": Pascal, *Pensées,* no. 126, p. 118 (English: no. 136, p. 67).

p. 51 "in complete idleness to commune with itself": Montaigne, *Essays,* p. 27.

p. 52 Rather than face the contingency of my existence, I flee it: This notion of existential flight is based on ideas in Heidegger's *Being and Time,* in particular those of falling and thrownness (section 38, pp. 219ff). It is treated at greater length in Batchelor, *Flight.*

p. 54 Fear is the longing not to be hurt: Despite the widespread use of the term "fear" (*bhaya*) in the discourses, no Buddhist tradition provides an in-depth analysis or definition of fear. Fear is not treated as a discrete mental event (*cetasika*) in any of the classical works of Abhidhamma. While it is sometimes regarded as an aspect of hatred (*dosa/dvesa*), I suggest that it is better understood as a kind of craving (*tanha/trsna*).

p. 54 fear pervades all self-centered emotion: Tibetan texts compare confusion's fear to an ox, arrogance's fear to a lion, hatred's fear to a fire, jealousy's fear to a snake, misconception's fear to a thief, miserliness' fear to an iron shackle, desire's fear to a torrent, doubt's fear to a cannibal. The fear implicit in these emotions suggests how each is animated by the longing not to be hurt. This list of the eight fears likewise affirms that fear is more than just a feature of hatred. See Rigzin Tsepak, *Tibetan-English Dictionary of Buddhist Terminology,* p. 87.

p. 54 "Mara conjured up his host": Quoted in Boyd, *Satan and Mara,* pp. 85–6. The *Mahavastu* is a relatively late Sanskrit text included in the canon of the Mahasamghika school.

p. 54 "The less the sage feared the frightful hosts": Ashvaghosa, *Buddhacarita,* XIII.55.

p. 54 "The eternal silence of these infinite spaces": Pascal, *Pensées,* no. 187, p. 161 (English: no. 201, p. 95).

pp. 55–56 "work out your own salvation with fear and trembling": Philippians 2.12.

p. 56 For Tsong-kha-pa, writing in Tibet: Tsong-kha-pa (1357–1419) was the founder of the Geluk school of Tibetan Buddhism. This assertion is found in *Great Treatise on the Stages of the Path to Enlightenment,* p. 179.

p. 56 "in order to arouse fear, trepidation and terror": See, for example, SN I.4.2 and 3, p. 196.

p. 57 "Though a hundred thousand rogues just like you": SN I.5.5, pp. 225–6.

p. 57 The fantasy . . . is both an anxious flight: For a further discussion of fixation, see Batchelor, *Verses from the Center,* pp. 61–3.

7. The Devil's Circle

p. 60 A disciple once found the Sufi sage Mullah Nasruddin: Quoted from memory.

p. 60 "Live like a milk-sucking baby": SN I.4.9, p. 201.

p. 61 "Everything . . . endeavors to persevere in its own being": From the third book of Spinoza's *Ethics,* quoted in Russell, *History of Western Philosophy,* p. 572.

p. 62 The troops under Mara's control: See p. 19 for a complete list of the ten "armies" of Mara.

p. 62 Buddha refused to be drawn on the question: These are among the fourteen questions Buddha refused to answer; see, for example, MN 63.2, p. 533. The fact that Buddha used the terms *jiva* (soul/life force) and *sarira* (body) in these passages suggests that the now familiar split between mind (*citta*) and matter (*rupa*) was not a dominant distinction for those to whom the discourses in the early canon were addressed. Later Buddhist traditions, however, inclined toward a body-mind dualism, in part due to the buddhological need to explain the process of rebirth.

8. A Devil in the Way

p. 65 "Mara—the enemy of freedom": Ashvaghosa, *Buddhacarita,* XIII.2, p. 137.

p. 65 "A devil is anything that obstructs the achievement of freedom": Quoted in Harding, *Machik's Complete Explanation,* p. 117.

p. 65 "can be known here and now": Sn 5.4.1053, p. 121.

p. 65 "The safe and good path that leads to happiness": MN 19.25–6, p. 210.

p. 65 "saddled his ass and went with the princes of Moab": Numbers 22.21.

p. 66 "one who throws something across one's path": Pagels, *Origin of Satan,* p. 39. Also see Arvind Sharma's essay on Satan in *Encyclopedia of Religion,* edited by Eliade, vol. 15, pp. 81–2.

p. 66 "hath fenced up my way that I cannot pass": Job 19.8.

p. 66 The Acts of the Apostles: Cf. Geering, *Christianity Without God,* p. 129. The passages noted by Geering are: Acts 9.2, 18.25, 19.23, 22.4, 24.14.

p. 66 "I will waylay Your servants" Koran 7.11*ff.*

p. 66 "Heaven and earth are ruthless . . . Lord of Slaughter": Lao-tzu, *Tao-te-ching* 5, p. 147; 74, p. 234.

p. 67 "If I think well of my life": Chuang-tzu, *Basic Writings,* p. 76.

p. 67 "become entangled with everything they meet": Ibid., p. 32.

p. 67 "running one's course like a galloping steed": Ibid., p. 33.

p. 67 "He can commit an error and not regret it": Ibid., p. 73.

p. 67 "puts himself in the background . . . benefits the ten thousand creatures": Lao-tzu, *Tao-te-ching* 7, p. 150; 8, p. 151.

p. 68 "ancient path traveled by the awakened ones of old": SN 12.65, p. 603.

9. *An Empty Space*

p. 71 "absence of resistance": In Tibetan, *thogs reg dgag rtsam gyi med dgag,* or more literally: "the simple negation which is the mere cessation of obstructive contact." This is the standard definition of "uncompounded space" (*dus ma byas kyi nam mkha*) in the Geluk school of Tibetan Buddhism. Such space is a negation and as such cannot be imagined as a thing of any kind. If a fence were put across a room, it would eliminate the lack of resistance at the point where it stands. But nothing would have to be removed to make way for it. Space has added significance in serving as the classic example of a "simple negation" (*med dgag*), i.e., a negation that does not imply the presence of anything else, which is also for the Geluk a defining feature of emptiness (*sunyata*).

p. 72 By contrast, in Sanskrit the noun *pratipad:* I am indebted to Jenny Wilks for this example.

p. 72 "obstructed" by the devil of compulsions: The Tibetan for the Sanskrit *kleshavarana* is *nyon mongs kyi sgrib pa,* which literally translates as the "obstruction which is compulsion." Only by overcoming this obstruction does one actually enter the path.

p. 73 "bands of thieves": BCA 5.27–9. In a different context, Jesus describes the function of the devil in a similar way: "then cometh the wicked one and catcheth away that which was sown in the heart," Matthew 13.19.

p. 74 "As soon as I know the mind is distorted": BCA 5.34.

p. 75 For the . . . Indian philosopher Nagarjuna, such contingency *is* emptiness: MMK 24.18. See Batchelor, *Verses from the Center,* pp. 20–1 and 124.

10. From Home to Homelessness

p. 77 "In a home . . . life is stifled in an atmosphere of dust": Sn 3.1, 406. Cf. Nanamoli, *Life of the Buddha,* p. 11.

p. 77 "The foxes have holes": Matthew 8.20.

p. 78 "Narrow is the way": Matthew 7.14.

p. 78 Buddha recognized that it was not enough: "This noble truth of the path leading to the cessation of suffering is to be developed," SN 5.56.11, p. 1845.

p. 79 As Ch'an (Zen) Buddhism evolved in China: Although the origins of Ch'an in China are traced to Bodhidharma in the sixth century, I refer here to the period from the Sixth Patriarch Hui-neng (638–713) onward when the tradition became widespread. The dispute between the advocates of "gradual" and "sudden" paths is a well-known feature of Zen lore, but modern scholarship suggests that the differences between these factions were considerably exaggerated for sectarian reasons. The distinction nonetheless sheds valuable light on the metaphor of the path. See McRae, *Northern School.*

p. 80 The path is more than just a task and a gift: This analysis of the path into three components—a goal, unobstructed movement, and a bond with others—corresponds to the threefold refuge in Buddhism. Taking refuge in Buddha is to commit oneself to the goal of the path of awakening; taking refuge in the Dharma is to commit oneself to treading the path itself; taking refuge in the Sangha is to commit oneself to those who inspire and accompany one on the path.

11. What Is This Thing?

p. 83 "Where did you come from?" asked Hui-neng: This encounter between Hui-neng and Huai-jang is the basis for the practice of the koan "What is this?" as taught in the Son (Zen) monasteries of Korea. It is cited, for example, in Buswell, *Korean Approach to Zen,* p. 37. For an account of the historical role of "What is this?" in China's Ch'an tradition, see Batchelor, *Faith to Doubt,* pp. 26–35. For a philosophical reflection on this kind of questioning as the foundation of religious consciousness, see Nishitani, *Religion and Nothingness,* pp. 1–45.

p. 83 Zen master Dogen declared Hui-neng's "What is this thing?": This is found in the *Bussho* fascicle of Dogen's *Shobogenzo,* cited in Abe, *Zen and Western Thought,* p. 37.

p. 84 "that is, when a man is capable of being in uncertainties": Keats, *Letters,* p. 43.

p. 85 According to legend: In Buddha's own account of his life before his awakening (MN 26), this well-known story of the renunciation is not mentioned. Buddha does, however, recount it in DN 14, when telling his followers of the life of the former Buddha Vipassi. Since this discourse describes the characteristic features of the lives of all those who become Buddhas, it implies that, in outline at least, Gotama likewise underwent a similar sequence of experiences prior to awakening. Such a story is better treated as myth than biography.

p. 85 "From now on, as soon as a hint of desire": Cited by Foucher, *La Vie du Bouddha,* p. 155; and Warren, *Buddhism in Translation,* p. 64. I follow Foucher here. I have been unable to trace the canonical source. Thanks to Sarah Harding for this reference.

p. 86 "If you meet Buddha . . . kill him": LC, p. 25.

p. 86 "Because it is so very close": Cleary, translator, *Swampland Flowers,* p. 71.

12. The Riddle of the World

p. 87 The words on this page: The scientific information in the following paragraphs is taken from: Maddox, *What Remains to be Discovered;* Rees, *Just Six Numbers;* Damasio, *Descartes' Error,* Gould, *Wonderful Life;* Fortey, *Life: An Unauthorised Biography;* Ehrlich, *Human Natures;* and Diamond, *Guns, Germs and Steel.*

p. 89 "improbable and fragile entity": Gould, *Wonderful Life,* p. 319.

p. 92 "look solid . . . but they are as fluid as ripples on a stream": Weiner, *Beak of the Finch,* pp. 88 and 111.

13. On Being Conscious

p. 95 "The fire is at its last click": Keats, *Letters,* p. 223.

p. 96 "the Photograph . . . is . . . the sovereign Contingency": Barthes, *La Chambre Claire,* p. 15 (English: *Camera Lucida,* p. 4).

p. 97 "the size of a grain of sand": Ramachandran and Blakeslee, *Phantoms in the Brain,* p. 8.

p. 98 Buddhism describes consciousness of the summer sky: Later Buddhist traditions developed forms of meditational practice (such as *mahamudra, dzogchen,* and Zen) that claim to lead to direct, nonconceptual insight into the nature of "Mind." While tending to avoid the word "consciousness" (*vijnana/rnam shes*) in favor of "primordial awareness" (*jnana/ye shes*), "knowing" (*vidya/rig pa*), or "Mind" (*citta/sems/hsin*), these systems talk of an immaterial, transcendent mode of pure knowing that can be accessed by direct subjective experience. Such language is, however, largely alien to the discourses attributed to the historical Buddha in the Pali Canon. For a critique of the scientific materialist view of consciousness as an emergent property of the brain and an account of these practices as offering a systematic approach to legitimate insights into the nature of consciousness, see Wallace, *Taboo of Subjectivity.*

14. This Body Is Breathing

p. 103 "ordinary men are deluded": From Chinul, *Straight Talk on the True Mind,* in Buswell, *The Korean Approach to Zen: The Collected Works of Chinul,* pp. 167, 162.

p. 104 "The way . . . is in the ant": Chuang-tzu, in Waley, *Three Ways of Thought in Ancient China,* p. 79.

p. 105 "If, possessed of such a body": Sn 1.11.206, p. 21. Although the contemplation of the "foulness" of the body is often presented as a monastic strategy to overcome feelings of sensuous desire, Buddha includes it among the foundations of mindfulness as one of the means to understand life as it is, thereby leading to the realization of nirvana. See MN 10, pp. 145–149. In Tantric Buddhist iconography, the skeleton is an explicit symbol of selflessness.

p. 106 "the direct path . . . for the attainment of the true way": MN 10.2, p. 145.

p. 106 "to the forest, to the root of a tree": MN 43.33, p. 394.

p. 107 Breathing meditation renders you intimately aware: For another account of this practice, see Batchelor, *Buddhism Without Beliefs,* pp. 23–6 and 62–5. The canonical source of this passage is MN 118.15–22, pp. 943–4; see also SN 5.54, pp. 1765–87.

p. 109 Just as the flame of a candle: This image combines an analogy found in Hui-neng, *Platform Sutra of the Sixth Patriarch,* section 15, p. 137, with oral meditation instructions in Tibetan Buddhism.

15. Learning to Wait

p. 112 "Do you know who it is . . . right there before your eyes": LC, p. 29. Lin-chi concludes this passage: "If a man has no faith [in this], he'll waste his entire life."

p. 113 "What is the purpose of nirvana?": SN 3.23.1, pp. 984–5. This passage begins with a discussion of Mara. See also the translator's footnote 243, pp. 1093–4.

p. 113 Whether it crystallizes into a question: On the Zen question (Korean: *hwadu*) "What is this?" see Batchelor, *Faith to Doubt,* pp. 26–35. The Korean Zen tradition compares the sensation of doubt that emerges from such questioning to the coagulation of milk. Teachers likewise suggest that this sensation be located in the belly.

p. 114 "Whatever is contingent . . . is naturally at ease": MMK 7.16.

p. 114 "living beings are naturally nirvanic": BCA 9.103.

p. 114 You just wait in the abyss of perplexity: On waiting and expecting, see Batchelor, *Faith to Doubt,* pp. 46–7; Heidegger, *Gelassenheit,* p. 42. (English: *Discourse on Thinking,* p. 68); also Eliot, *Four Quartets,* "East Coker," *Collected Poems,* p. 200.

p. 115 "If you seek Buddha": LC, p. 21.

p. 115 sensual desire, ill-will, restlessness, torpor, and doubt: These are the classic five hindrances of Theravada Buddhism. This presentation of them follows SN 46.31–40, pp. 1589–93. Here the Buddha presents them as what are overcome by the seven factors of awakening: mindfulness, discrimination of states, energy, rapture, tranquility, concentration, and equanimity; "lead away from nirvana": SN 46.40, p. 1593; the mind quickly loses its natural suppleness and radiancy: See SN 46.33, p. 1590, where the Buddha compares the mind to gold and the hindrances to base metals that corrupt it; "encirclers of the mind": SN 46.39, p. 1593.

THREE: LIVING WITH THE DEVIL

16. An Ordinary Person's Life

p. 122 Rather than gaining insight: See Batchelor, *Buddhism Without Beliefs,* pp. 3–13, for a fuller account of awakening and the four truths.

p. 123 "I have stopped . . .": MN 86, pp. 711–2.

p. 123 "How dare these southern devils say": Ferguson, *Zen's Chinese Heritage,* p. 196–7. I have also incorporated some of the wording of this story from Cleary and Cleary, *Blue Cliff Record,* vol. 1, p. 24.

p. 125 "What is awakening?": Ferguson, *Zen's Chinese Heritage,* pp. 198–9.

p. 126 "In this lump of raw flesh": LC, p. 3; Kasulis, *Zen Action Zen Person,* p. 51. My translation has been further checked against the Chinese by Martine Batchelor.

17. *"Do Not Hurt Me"*

p. 130 A core paradox of human existence: This is the central theme explored in Batchelor, *Alone with Others*.

p. 131 "he is not a point in the world net of space and time": Buber, *Ich und Du,* p. 15 (English: *I and Thou,* p. 59).

p. 131 "The first word of the face": Levinas, *Ethics and Infinity,* p. 89. I am indebted to this idea of Levinas for inspiring much of what is written in this section of the book.

p. 132 "do not kill me, do not rob me": This is a Levinasian restatement of the Buddhist doctrine of the ten unwholesome actions (Pali: *akusala kamma patha*).

p. 132 These pleas are the foundation of an ethics: Avoiding the ten unwholesome actions is to observe a "natural morality" (Tibetan: *rang bzhin gyi kha na ma tho ba*), while refraining from what is prohibited by lay, monastic, bodhisattva, or tantric precepts is to observe an "entailed morality" (Tibetan: *bcas kyi kha na ma tho ba*).

18. *The Anguish of Others*

p. 136 "For I was hungry, and ye gave me meat": Matthew 25.35–6, 40.

p. 137 "the mind reaches a stage": Thurman, *Holy Teaching of Vimalakirti,* pp. 164–5.

p. 137 "Why does the hand protect the foot": BCA 8.99.

p. 137 "If the foot could speak": From the sermon "See What Love," translated in Schürmann, *Meister Eckhart,* p. 132. This ancient metaphor of the body and its parts was used by Paul in I Corinthians 12 as a way of describing the Body of Christ, to which Eckhart is alluding in this sermon.

p. 138 "When someone steps on another's foot": Quoted in Schür-mann, ibid., p. 153.

p. 138 "This separated member believes itself": Pascal, *Pensées,* no. 352, p. 227 (English: no. 372, pp. 136–7). As with Eckhart, Pascal is also commenting on I Corinthians.

p. 139 "is just like feeding oneself": BCA 8.116.

19. Incarnation

p. 142 "At that instant . . . drowning in the charmlessness of the body": Kundera, *Immortality,* p. 3. I have modified the second sentence in accordance with the French translation: *Sa main s'était envolée avec une ravissante légèreté.* Given the importance of sensuality and lightness in the Kunderan universe, the English "bewitching ease" seems unsatis-factory.

p. 144 "is a material vestige of its subject": Sontag, *On Photography,* p. 154.

p. 144 "All novels are concerned with the enigma of self": Kundera, *The Art of the Novel,* pp. 23, 31, 25, 28. Tereza is a central character of Kundera's novel *The Unbearable Lightness of Being.*

p. 145 "This dharma I have attained is profound": MN 26.19, p. 260.

p. 145 "with little dust in their eyes who are wasting": MN 26.20, p. 261. For the sake of simplicity, I have called this god "Brahma," whereas the text refers to him as "Brahma Sahampati." In Buddhist polytheistic cosmology, "Brahma" denotes a class of gods who inhabit the realm of pure form (*rupaloka*). Buddha encounters several gods from this realm in the discourses, each of whom has a specific name. Yet they all share in common the tendency to inflation, which manifests itself in believing themselves to be the greatest of Brahmas, i.e., God. Throughout the canon, Buddha ridicules this claim, either by demonstrating his superior knowledge or by caricaturing them as fools who mindlessly repeat their claim without understanding what it means. See MN 49 and DN 11.

p. 147 "Mara took possession of a member of the god's assembly": MN 49.5, p. 425. This Brahma is called "Baka."

p. 147 "I know you, Evil One": MN 49.6, pp. 425–6.

p. 149 "who *speaks* is not who *writes*": Quoted by Susan Sontag, "In Jerusalem," *New York Review of Books,* June 21, 2001, p. 22.

p. 149 "It's Borges, the other one": Borges, *Collected Fictions,* p. 324.

20. A Culture of Awakening

p. 152 "Wander forth, O monks, for the welfare of the multitude": A commonly cited refrain. See, for example, SN 1.4.5, p. 198. The final sentence is not italicized in the original translation.

p. 152 "The sage who wanders alone is like the wind": Sn 1.12.213, p. 23.

p. 153 "hemmed in . . . set off alone, without a companion": *Udana* IV.5, *Naga Sutta.*

p. 153 "To become independent of others": This phrase is used to describe one who has become a "stream entrant" (*sotapanna*), i.e., has gained direct experiential insight into the four ennobling truths and embarked on the eightfold path.

p. 154 "send some men to take the monk Gotama's life": Nanamoli, *Life of the Buddha,* p. 261. The story of Devadatta is found in chapter 7 of the Cullavagga of the Vinaya (monastic rule) section of the Pali Canon.

p. 155 "bodily feelings that were painful, sharp, racking": Ibid., p. 263. See also Buddha. SN 4. 13, p. 203.

p. 155 "Mara came to him and addressed him in verse": Ibid.

p. 155 "a wastrel, a clot of spittle": Ibid., p. 259.

p. 155 Devadatta now conspired to create a schism: This discussion follows ibid., pp. 266–8.

p. 156 "For where God built a church": From Luther, *Colloquia Mensalia,* ch. 2.

p. 156 "And the devil did grin, for his darling sin": This poem, originally co-written with Robert Southey, was first published on September 6, 1799, in the *Morning Post and Gazetteer.* It was revised by Southey in 1827 and Coleridge in 1829 and 1835.

p. 156 "Through aping me": Nanamoli, *Life of the Buddha,* pp. 271, 270.

p. 157 Buddha did not refuse him because he had someone better qualified in mind: See ibid., p. 259, where Buddha replies to Devadatta's request to turn over control of the community, "I would not hand over the community of bhikkhus even to Sariputta or Mogallana. How should I do so to such a wastrel, a clot of spittle, as you?"

p. 158 "grass, twigs, branches and leaves" and following quotations: MN 22, p. 228.

p. 158 Rather than preaching an ideology: This principle finds classic expression in the *Kalama Sutta* as well as in the oft-quoted example of testing what Buddha taught with the same thoroughness as a goldsmith tests a metal to see if it is gold. Although Gotama did not make a formal distinction between an "idea" and an "ideology," his ambiguous use of the term *ditthi* ("view"), which he uses approvingly as in "right view" but disapprovingly as in "the thicket of views," suggests an awareness of how even liberating views can harden into obstructive opinions. A striking contrast exists between the suggestive but technically imprecise way in which Buddha speaks of meditation practice in the early discourses, and the highly technical manner it is presented in the meditation manuals of many contemporary Buddhist schools.

p. 159 to paraphrase Max Weber, the routinization of awakening: Weber spoke of the "routinization of charisma" as a stage through which religions pass as they move from being anarchic, charismatic movements to established churches.

21. The Kingdom of Mara

p. 162 Bimbisara is presented as a powerful but humane ruler: Cf. Nanamoli, *Life of the Buddha,* pp. 67–9.

p. 162 "Formerly, men were long-lived, now they are short-lived": Ibid., pp. 260–1.

p. 163 "felt fear and terror and his hair stood on end": DN 2.10, p. 92.

p. 163 "Since you have acknowledged the transgression and confessed": DN 2.99, p. 108.

p. 163 "The king is done for, his fate is sealed": DN 2.102, p. 109.

p. 164 "who are intoxicated with sovereignty": SN 3. 25, p. 192.

p. 164 On hearing of Pasenadi's battles: See SN 3.14–15, pp. 178–9; Nor does Buddha disapprove: SN 3.11, pp. 173–4; On learning that a great animal sacrifice is being prepared: SN 3.9, pp. 171–2; "a great mass of people . . . concern for wives and children": SN 3.10, p. 172.

p. 165 The only time his behavior is seen to be changed: SN 3.13, pp. 176–7; 3.25, p. 193.

p. 166 "If I reprimand [the king] for such a terrible deed": SN 1, p. 410, fn. 257. The translator, Bhikkhu Bodhi, argues that "the story does not fit well, and I would add that it even detracts from the solemn dignity of the Buddha's discourses."

p. 166 "And now we depart": MN 89.20, p. 733. This discourse (the *Dhammacetiya Sutta*) recounts in detail the last meeting between Pasenadi and Buddha but only hints at the events that follow. The events of Buddha's final months are told in the *Discourse on the Great Passing (Mahaparinibbana Sutta)* (DN 16, pp. 230–77). For other historical material I have followed Lamotte, *History of Indian Buddhism,* pp. 11–12.

p. 167 "miserable little wattle-and-daub town": DN 16.5.17, p. 266.

p. 168 "I am a Kosalan and you are a Kosalan": MN 89.20, p. 733.

p. 168 "I shall not enter final nirvana": Although this episode with Mara does not appear as such in the Pali Canon, it is preserved in the Sanskrit Canon of the Mulasarvastivadin school, in chapter 4 of the *Catushparishat Sutra.* The episode is referred to, however, in DN 16.3.34–5, pp. 250–1, where the passage cited here also appears in full. Thanks to Jenny Wilks for this information and the translation from Sanskrit.

22. Hearing the Cries

p. 170 the consul Menenius Agrippa: See Schürmann, *Meister Eckhart,* p. 153, who says of this doctrine: "Ever since [Agrippa], it has served to justify bondage under corporations and established hierarchies." See also Popper, *Open Society and Its Enemies,* I, p. 294. This episode likewise serves as the opening of Shakespeare's tragedy *Coriolanus* (Act 1, scene 1).

p. 170 "His mouth became the Brahmin": O'Flaherty, *Rig Veda* (X.90.11–12), p. 30.

p. 171 When Shantideva uses this same organicist metaphor: For the use of this metaphor by Shantideva, Eckhart, and Pascal, see above, pp. 137–8.

p. 171 In the light of modern biology: I am indebted to biologist Mark Mescher for these examples.

p. 173 "the organ of hearing to quiet the mind": Lu K'uan Yu, *Surangama Sutra,* p. 142. This discourse is attributed to Buddha but is understood by modern scholars as an apocryphal text composed in Chinese. See also Batchelor, *Faith to Doubt,* pp. 47–9.

p. 175 "Freedom consists in being able to do whatever": Morange, *La Déclaration des Droits de l'Homme,* p. 118.

p. 177 "No one is born a brahmin": Sn 3.9.650–2, p. 75.

23. The Anarchy of the Gaps

p. 180 "If the doors of perception were cleansed": Blake, *Marriage of Heaven and Hell,* plate 14.

p. 181 The Sanskrit term translated as "nature" is *garbha:* The Sanskrit for "buddhanature" is either *tathagatagarbha* ("womb of the tathagata") or *buddhagotra* ("buddha lineage") or *buddhadhatu* ("buddha element"). There is no exact Sanskrit equivalent of "buddhanature." (Note that in the Pali Canon none of these terms are ever used.) The English "buddhanature" has gained currency due to the Chinese translation of the Sanskrit terms as *fo-shing* ("buddha-nature"). For further details see King, *Buddha Nature,* pp. 3–5 and 173–4.

p. 181 the Pali term *appamada,* which can be translated as "care": This term is variously translated as "diligence," "heedfulness," "vigilance," "zeal," "conscientiousness." Ernst Steinkellner, in his German translation of Shantideva's *Guide,* opts for *wachsame Sorge,* which would translate as "watchful (or wakeful) care." See BCA 4 for Shantideva's treatment of care.

p. 182 "The careful do not die": *Dhammapada,* v. 21, p. 38.

p. 182 "Conditions are subject to decay": DN 16.6.7, p. 270. This final sentence was translated by T. W. Rhys Davids (following Paul's letter to the Philippians 2.12) as "Work out your salvation with diligence," and subsequently cited by T. S. Eliot in his play *The Cocktail Party* (Act 2). Maurice Walshe renders it "strive on untiringly"; Nanamoli has "Attain perfection through diligence." Another rendition might be "Accomplish everything with care."

p. 182 Buddhist analyses of care describe: I am here drawing on Mahayana sources based on Asanga's *Abhidharmasamuccaya*. See Rabten, *Mind and Its Functions*, p. 133.

p. 182 "a keen concern for engagement and letting go": Zangpo, *Legs par bshad pa'i rgya mtsho*, p. 56.

p. 183 "always to be a student of everyone": BCA 5.74.

p. 183 "There is nothing whatsoever that is not to be learned": BCA 5.100.

p. 185 "The world was all before them": Milton, *Paradise Lost*, Book XII, lines 656–9.

BIBLIOGRAPHY

Not all the texts listed here are cited in this book. I have included a number of works that I either consulted or read in the course of the writing that in one way or another helped shape the narrative.

Abe, Masao. *Zen and Western Thought*. Edited by William Lafleur. London: Macmillan, 1985.

Ashvaghosa. *Buddhacarita*. E. B. Cowell, translator, in *Buddhist Mahayana Texts* [1894]. Delhi: Motilal Banarsidass, 1974.

Barthes, Roland. *La Chambre Claire: Notes sur la Photographie*. Paris: Le Seuil, 1980. English: Richard Howard, translator. *Camera Lucida: Reflections on Photography*. London: Vintage, 2000.

Batchelor, Stephen. *Alone with Others: An Existential Approach to Buddhism*. New York: Grove, 1983.

———. *The Awakening of the West: The Encounter of Buddhism and Western Culture*. Berkeley: Parallax, 1994.

————. *Buddhism Without Beliefs: A Contemporary Guide to Awakening.* New York: Riverhead, 1996.

————. *The Faith to Doubt: Glimpses of Buddhist Uncertainty.* Berkeley: Parallax, 1990.

————. *Flight: An Existential Conception of Buddhism.* Kandy: Buddhist Publication Society, 1984.

————. *Verses from the Center: A Buddhist Vision of the Sublime.* New York: Riverhead, 2000.

Baudelaire, Charles. *Les Fleurs du Mal* (1861 ed.). Edited by Claude Pichois. Paris: Gallimard, 1996.

Baudrillard, Jean. *La Transparence du Mal.* Paris: Galilée, 1990. English: James Benedict, translator. *The Transparency of Evil.* London: Verso, 1993.

Beckett, Samuel. *Stories and Texts for Nothing.* New York: Grove, 1967.

Berlin, Isaiah. *Four Essays on Liberty.* Oxford: Oxford University Press, 1969.

Blackmore, Susan. *The Meme Machine.* New York: Oxford University Press, 1999.

Blake, William. *The Marriage of Heaven and Hell.* Introduction and commentary by Sir Geoffrey Keynes. Oxford: Oxford University Press, 1975.

Blanchot, Maurice. *The Space of Literature.* Translated by Ann Smock. [1955] Lincoln: University of Nebraska Press, 1982.

Borg, Marcus, editor. *Jesus and Buddha: The Parallel Sayings.* Berkeley: Seastone, 1997.

Borges, Jorge Luis. *Collected Fictions.* Translated by Andrew Hurley. New York: Penguin, 1998.

Boyd, James W. *Satan and Mara: Christian and Buddhist Symbols of Evil.* Leiden: E. J. Brill, 1975.

Buber, Martin. *Ich und Du*. Heidelberg: Lambert Schneider, 1979. English: Walter Kaufmann, translator. *I and Thou*. Edinburgh: T. & T. Clark, 1970.

Buddha. *The Connected Discourses of the Buddha: A New Translation of the Samyutta Nikaya*. 2 vols. Translated by Bhikkhu Bodhi. Boston: Wisdom Publications, 2000.

————. *The Dhammapada*. Translated by Juan Mascaro. London and New York: Penguin, 1973.

————. *The Long Discourses of the Buddha: A Translation of the Digha Nikaya*. Translated by Maurice Walshe. Boston: Wisdom Publications, 1987.

————. *The Middle Length Discourses of the Buddha: A New Translation of the Majjhima Nikaya*. Translated by Bhikkhu Nanamoli and Bhikkhu Bodhi. Boston: Wisdom Publications, 1995.

————. *The Sutta-Nipata*. Translated by H. Saddhatissa. London: Curzon, 1994.

————. *The Udana: Inspired Utterances of the Buddha*. Translated by John D. Ireland. Kandy: Buddhist Publication Society, 1997.

Buswell, Robert E. *The Korean Approach to Zen: The Collected Works of Chinul*. Honolulu: University of Hawaii Press, 1983.

Chuang-Tzu. *Basic Writings*. Translated by Burton Watson. New York: Columbia University Press, 1964.

Cleary, Christopher, translator. *Swampland Flowers: The Letters and Lectures of Zen Master Ta-hui*. New York: Grove, 1977.

Cleary, Thomas, and J. C. Cleary. *The Blue Cliff Record*. Boulder and London: Shambhala, 1977.

Comte-Sponville, André. *Présentations de la Philosophie*. Paris: Albin Michel, 2000.

Conze, Edward, translator and editor. *Buddhist Scriptures*. London: Penguin, 1959.

————. *The Large Sutra on Perfect Wisdom: With the Divisions of the Ab-hisamayalamkara.* Berkeley: University of California Press, 1975.

Cupitt, Don. *Emptiness and Brightness.* Santa Rosa, CA: Polebridge, 2001.

————. *The Time Being.* London: SCM, 1992.

Damasio, Antonio R. *Descartes' Error: Emotion, Reason and the Human Brain.* London: Picador, 1995.

Dante. *The Divine Comedy.* Vol. I: *Inferno.* Translated by Mark Musa. New York: Penguin Classics, 1984.

Dawkins, Richard. *River Out of Eden.* London: Phoenix, 1995.

————. *The Selfish Gene.* Oxford: Oxford University Press, 1976.

————. *Unweaving the Rainbow: Science, Delusion and the Appetite for Wonder.* London: Penguin, 1998.

Dennett, Daniel. C. *Darwin's Dangerous Idea: Evolution and the Meanings of Life.* New York: Simon & Schuster, 1995.

————. *Freedom Evolves.* New York: Viking, 2003.

Diamond, Jared. *Guns, Germs and Steel: A Short History of Everybody for the Last 13,000 Years.* London: Vintage, 1998.

Dreyfus, Georges B. J. *Recognizing Reality: Dharmakirti's Philosophy and Its Tibetan Interpretations.* Albany: SUNY Press, 1997.

Ehrlich, Paul. *Human Natures: Genes, Cultures, and the Human Prospect.* New York: Penguin, 2002.

Eliade, Mircea, editor. *The Encyclopedia of Religion.* New York: Macmillan, 1987.

Eliot, T. S. *Collected Poems 1909–1962.* London: Faber and Faber, 1963.

Fortey, Richard. *Life: An Unauthorised Biography.* London: Harper-Collins, 1997.

Foucher, A. *La Vie du Bouddha.* Paris: Adrien Maisonneuve, 1993.

Gampopa. *Jewel Ornament of Liberation.* Translated by Herbert V. Guenther. London: Rider, 1970.

Garfield, Jay L. *The Fundamental Wisdom of the Middle Way: Nagarjuna's* Mulamadhyamakakarika. New York: Oxford University Press, 1995.

Geering, Lloyd. *Christianity Without God*. Santa Rosa, CA: Polebridge, 2002.

Gould, Stephen Jay. *Wonderful Life: The Burgess Shale and the Nature of History*. New York: Norton, 1989.

Gray, John. *Straw Dogs: Thoughts on Humans and Other Animals*. London: Granta, 2002.

Gribben, John. *Stardust*. London: Penguin, 2000.

Guenther, Herbert V. *The Life and Teachings of Naropa*. Boston: Shambhala, 1986.

Harding, Sarah. *Machik's Complete Explanation: Clarifying the Meaning of Chöd*. Ithaca, NY: Snow Lion, 2003.

Heidegger, Martin. *Being and Time*. Translated by John Macquarrie and Edward Robinson. Oxford: Basil Blackwell, 1978.

———. *Gelassenheit*. Pfullingen: Neske, 1959. English: John M. Anderson and E. Hans Freund, translators. *Discourse on Thinking: A Translation of* Gelassenheit. New York: Harper & Row, 1966.

Hitchens, Christopher. *Letters to a Young Contrarian*. New York: Basic Books, 2001.

Horgan, John. *The End of Science*. London: Abacus, 1998.

———. *The Undiscovered Mind*. New York: Free Press, 1999.

Hui-neng. *The Platform Sutra of the Sixth Patriarch*. Translated by Philip B. Yampolsky. New York: Columbia University Press, 1967.

Jaynes, Julian. *The Origin of Consciousness in the Breakdown of the Bicameral Mind*. New York: Houghton Mifflin, 1990.

Kafka, Franz. *The Trial*. Translated by Willa and Edwin Muir. London: Penguin, 1953.

Kasulis, T. P. *Zen Action Zen Person*. Honolulu: University of Hawaii Press, 1981.

Keats, John. *Letters of John Keats*. Edited by Robert Gittings. Oxford: Oxford University Press, 1970.

Kerr, Fergus. *Theology after Wittgenstein*. Oxford: Basil Blackwell, 1986.

Kershaw, Ian. *Hitler: 1889–1936: Hubris,* vol. I. London: Penguin, 1999.

King, Sallie B. *Buddha Nature*. Albany: SUNY Press, 1991.

Kundera, Milan. *L'Art du Roman*. Paris: Gallimard, 1986. English: Linda Asher, translator. *The Art of the Novel*. New York: Grove, 1988.

———. *L'Immortalité*. Paris: Gallimard, 1990. English: Peter Kussi, translator. *Immortality*. London: Faber and Faber, 1991.

Lamotte, Etienne. *History of Indian Buddhism*. Translated by Sara Webb-Boin. Louvain and Paris: Peeters Press, 1988.

Lao-tzu. *Tao-te-ching. The Way and Its Power: A Study of the Tao Te Ching and Its Place in Chinese Thought*. Translated by Arthur Waley. New York: Grove, 1958.

Lawson, Hilary. *Closure: A Story of Everything*. London: Routledge, 2001.

Levinas, Emmanuel. *Ethics and Infinity: Conversations with Philippe Nemo*. Translated by Richard A. Cohen. Pittsburgh: Duquesne University Press, 1985.

Lewis, C. S. *The Screwtape Letters*. [1942] London: HarperCollins, 2001.

Lin-chi. *The Record of Lin-chi*. Translated by Ruth Fuller Sazaki. Kyoto: Institute for Zen Studies, 1975.

Ling, T. O. *The Buddha*. London: Temple Smith, 1973.

———. *Buddhism and the Mythology of Evil*. London: George Allen and Unwin, 1962.

Lu K'uan Yu (Charles Luk), translator. *The Surangama Sutra*. London: Rider, 1966.

McRae, John R. *The Northern School and the Formation of Early Ch'an Buddhism.* Honolulu: Hawaii University Press, 1986.

Maddox, John. *What Remains to Be Discovered.* New York: Free Press, 1998.

Milton, John. *Paradise Lost.* Edited by Christopher Ricks. London: Penguin, 1989.

Montaigne, Michel de. *Essays.* Translated by J. M. Cohen. London: Penguin, 1958.

Morange, Jean, editor. *La Déclaration des Droits de l'Homme et du Citoyen (26 août 1789).* Paris: PUF, 1988.

Nagarjuna. *Mula madhyamaka karika. (Verses from the Center)* Tibetan: L. P. Lhalungpa, editor. *dBu ma rtsa ba'i tshig le'ur byas pa shes rab ces bya ba.* Delhi, 1970. See also: *Woodblock to Laser* CD-ROM, Release A. Washington, D.C.: Asian Classics Input Project, 1993. Translated by Garfield (see above) and in poetic form by Batchelor (see above).

Nanamoli, Bhikkhu. *The Life of the Buddha.* Kandy: Buddhist Publication Society, 1978.

Nietzsche, Friedrich. *Ecce Homo.* Translated by R. J. Hollingdale. Harmondsworth and New York: Penguin, 1979.

Nishitani, Keiji. *Religion and Nothingness.* Translated by Jan van Bragt. Berkeley: University of California Press, 1982.

Nørretranders, Tor. *The User Illusion: Cutting Consciousness Down to Size.* New York: Penguin, 1999.

Nyanatiloka. *Buddhist Dictionary: Manual of Buddhist Terms and Doctrines.* 4th rev. ed. Kandy: Buddhist Publication Society, 1980.

O'Flaherty, Wendy Doniger. *The Origins of Evil in Hindu Mythology.* Berkeley: University of California Press, 1976.

―――, translator. *The Rig Veda.* London: Penguin, 1981.

Otto, Rudolf. *The Idea of the Holy.* Translated by John W. Harvey. London: Oxford University Press, 1958.

Pagels, Elaine. *The Origin of Satan.* New York: Vintage Books, 1996.

Pascal, Blaise. *Pensées.* Edited by Michel Le Guern. Paris: Gallimard, 1977. English: A. J. Krailsheimer, translator. *Pensées.* London: Penguin, 1966.

Popper, Karl R. *The Open Society and Its Enemies.* 2 vols. London: Routledge, 1966.

Rabten, Geshé. *The Mind and Its Functions.* Translated by Stephen Batchelor. Le Mont Pelerin: Editions Rabten, 1992.

Ramachandran, V. S., and Sandra Blakeslee. *Phantoms in the Brain: Human Nature and the Architecture of the Mind.* London: Fourth Estate, 1999.

Rees, Martin. *Just Six Numbers: The Deep Forces That Shape the Universe.* London: Weidenfeld & Nicolson, 1999.

Rigzin, Tsepak. *Tibetan-English Dictionary of Buddhist Terminology.* Dharamsala: Library of Tibetan Works and Archives, 1993.

Rorty, Richard. *Contingency, Irony and Solidarity.* Cambridge, England: Cambridge University Press, 1989.

Russell, Bertrand. *A History of Western Philosophy.* New York: Simon & Schuster, 1945.

Russell, Jeffrey Burton. *The Devil: Perceptions of Evil from Antiquity to Primitive Christianity.* Ithaca: Cornell University Press, 1977.

Schürmann, Reiner. *Meister Eckhart: Mystic and Philosopher.* Bloomington: Indiana University Press, 1978.

Shantideva. *A Guide to the Bodhisattva's Way of Life.* Translated by Stephen Batchelor. Dharamsala: LTWA, 1979. See also: *The Bodhicaryavatara.* Translated by Kate Crosby and Andrew Skilton. Oxford: Oxford University Press, 1995.

Sharma, Arvind. "The Devil." In Eliade, *The Encyclopedia of Religion* (see above).

Sontag, Susan. *On Photography.* New York: Penguin, 1977.

Thurman, Robert A. F., translator. *The Holy Teaching of Vimalakirti: A Mahayana Scripture.* University Park: Pennsylvania State University Press, 1976.

Tillich, Paul. *Systematic Theology.* 3 vols. in one. Chicago: University of Chicago Press, 1967.

Tsong-kha-pa. *The Great Treatise on the Stages of the Path to Enlightenment,* vol. I. Translated by Lamrim Chenmo Translation Committee. Ithaca, NY: Snow Lion, 2000.

Varela, Franciso J., Evan Thompson, and Eleanor Rosch. *The Embodied Mind: Cognitive Science and Human Experience.* Cambridge, MA: MIT Press, 1991.

Waley, Arthur. *Three Ways of Thought in Ancient China.* London: George Allen and Unwin, 1939.

———. *The Way and Its Power: A Study of the* Tao Te Ching *and Its Place in Chinese Thought.* New York: Grove, 1958.

Wallace, B. Alan. *The Taboo of Subjectivity: Toward a New Science of Consciousness.* New York: Oxford University Press, 2000.

Warren, Henry Clarke. *Buddhism in Translation.* Cambridge, MA: Harvard University Press, 1896.

Weiner, Jonathan. *The Beak of the Finch: A Story of Evolution in Our Time.* New York: Vintage, 1995.

Wilson, Edward O. *Consilience: The Unity of Knowledge.* London: Little, Brown, 1998.

Wittgenstein, Ludwig. *Philosophical Investigations.* Translated by G. E. M. Anscombe. Oxford: Blackwell, 1958.

Zangpo, Thogmé (Thogs med bzangs po). *Byang chub sems dpa'i spyod pa la 'jug pa la 'jug pa'i 'grel pa legs par bshad pa'i rgya mtsho.* Sarnath: Elegant Sayings, 1974.

Zeldin, Theodore. *An Intimate History of Humanity.* London: Vintage, 1998.

ACKNOWLEDGMENTS

Over the three years during which this book was written, a number of people, knowingly or otherwise, have left their mark on its pages. The work of the late Trevor Ling has been invaluable in my understanding of both Mara and Buddha. Bhikkhu Bodhi's magisterial translation of the *Samyutta Nikaya* (*Connected Discourses of the Buddha*) was published just as I began my research and has served as my primary canonical source. Don Cupitt's radical theology has had a growing influence on my work and has given me the courage to follow my own instincts in the interpretation of classical doctrines. The libretto for Philip Glass's Symphony No. 5 (compiled by Glass, James Parks Morton, and Kusumita P. Pedersen) confirmed how texts from very different sources can work together as a whole without compromising their integrity. Guy Claxton, Marjorie Silverman, Helen Tworkov, and Gay Watson read early drafts of the manuscript and offered suggestions that have improved the text. Robert Beer, Sarah Harding, and Jenny Wilks provided technical references, without which this book would have been poorer. Daniel Milles, Charles Genoud, and Gil Fronsdal unwittingly pointed me to textual passages that I subsequently used. Martine Batchelor gave me a copy of *Les Fleurs du Mal* and thereby brought Baudelaire into the narrative. Mark Mescher made a detailed critique of a late draft from an evolutionary biologist's perspective, which led to a number of significant changes. My agent, Anne Edelstein, has served as a gently supportive presence since the book's inception. By helping me see the architecture, symmetry, and density of the text, my editor, Amy Hertz, enabled it to reach its final form. All people, I have discovered, have a favorite anecdote or image that sums up their understanding of the devil. I neither recall nor have room to mention all those who have shared these with me, but I thank them for confirming my own intuitions as well as pointing me in unsuspected directions.

Aquitaine, France
December 2003

ABOUT THE AUTHOR

Stephen Batchelor was born in Scotland and trained as a monk in Buddhist monasteries in India, Switzerland, and Korea. He has translated and written several books on Buddhism, including *A Guide to the Bodhisattva's Way of Life* (Shantideva); *Alone with Others; The Faith to Doubt; The Awakening of the West; Buddhism Without Beliefs;* and *Verses from the Center* (Nagarjuna). He is a contributing editor to *Tricycle: The Buddhist Review;* a cofounder of Sharpham College for Buddhist Studies and Contemporary Enquiry; and a member of the teacher council of Gaia House meditation center. Batchelor, who lectures and conducts retreats worldwide, lives with his wife, Martine, in southwest France. Information on his work and teaching schedule are posted at www.stephenbatchelor.org.